Presented To:

_____

From:

_____

Date:

_____

SPIRIT
LIFE
TRAINING

SPIRIT LIFE TRAINING

IF YOU KNEW WHAT GOD HAS PUT WITHIN YOU,

YOU WOULD TRAIN IT TO BECOME

YOUR GREATEST ASSET

TIMOTHY JORGENSEN

DESTINY IMAGE® PUBLISHERS, INC.

P.O. Box 310, Shippensburg, PA 17257-0310

"Speaking to the Purposes of God for This Generation and for the Generations to Come."

Previously published as *Spirit Life Training* by instantpublisher.com.

This book and all other Destiny Image, Revival Press, MercyPlace, Fresh Bread, Destiny Image Fiction, and Treasure House books are available at Christian bookstores and distributors worldwide.

Previously published by instantpublisher.com ©2008
ISBN 978-1-60458-205-5

For a U.S. bookstore nearest you, call 1-800-722-6774.

For more information on foreign distributors, call 717-532-3040.

Reach us on the Internet: www.destinyimage.com.

ISBN 13 TP: 978-0-7684-3848-2

ISBN 13 Ebook: 978-0-7684-8973-6

For Worldwide Distribution, Printed in the U.S.A.

1 2 3 4 5 6 7 8 9 10 /15 14 13 12 11

ACKNOWLEDGMENTS

I would first like to thank a couple of ministers who have helped train me in these things—Roberts Liardon and Dr. Jonathan David. You both have been instrumental in imparting into my life and inspiring me to impact the nations of the world through this type of training.

I also thank brother Curry Blake of John G. Lake Ministries for his companionship as well as spiritual leadership. I appreciate his drive that the Word will always "become flesh" in our lives. There are real lives at stake, and the obedient choices we make based on the Word of God mean not only life and death for ourselves, but also for others who depend on us and our choices.

I also thank my wife, Rina. She has been a great training partner and a voice of God for encouragement and inspiration in my life. I love you very much!

ENDORSEMENTS

Tim Jorgensen's latest book, *Spirit Life Training,* reveals vital truths that will help you develop your spiritual life—a life that will be able to take any task God asks of you with confidence. He has proven these truths in his own life and knows how they work. When you read this powerful book, you will discover step-by-step teaching that will help anyone develop a strong spirit, among many other scripturally-based instructions on how to live a life of spiritual achievement.

ROBERTS LIARDON

Tim Jorgensen is a true man of God. He knows how to bring the Gospel in a way that anyone can understand it. He has the heart of David and the love of Jesus to see the Word of God spread to the uttermost parts of the world. He has a lot of wisdom, like the Bereans, and it shows in this book. I highly recommend Tim Jorgensen.

DR. JEREMY LOPEZ
Founder, Identity Network

Tim Jorgensen has been extremely instrumental in helping to shape my understanding of walking in the dominion of the spirit and not in the weakness of the flesh. Spirit Life Training is a very practical and powerful manual for how to overcome the battles that the enemy throws at every Christian. Tim has compiled years of wisdom into an easy-to-understand guide for those who are fed up with powerless, defeated, "religious" Christianity. He provides believers, new and old alike, with weapons to walk in the fullness of the victorious life that Christ offers all those who will "man-up" and go after living as the conquerors that He has made us to be.

RYAN J. RHOADES
Revival or Riots Ministries

In me is working a power stronger than every other power...the life that is in me is a thousand times bigger than I am outside.

—SMITH WIGGLESWORTH
"Life in the Spirit" (Sermon)

The spirit of man is God's divine dynamo. When you go to pray, your spirit gets into motion. Not ten thousand revolutions per minute, but possibly one hundred thousand. The voltage of heaven comes to your heart and flows from your hands, it burns into the souls of men and God Almighty's Spirit is applied through you to their need.

—JOHN G. LAKE
"The Science of Divine Healing" (Sermon)

CONTENTS

PART II—RELATIONSHIP WITH THE HOLY SPIRIT

FOREWORD

It is a great pleasure for me to endorse Tim's book, *Spirit Life Training*. Tim does a great job of detailing and defining the relationship and the cooperation of the Holy Spirit with our human spirits. I believe in the book so much that not only do we carry the book on our Website store page, but I have also made the book mandatory reading for all John G. Lake Ministries leadership and personnel. The study of the relationship of the Holy Spirit and our human spirits is quite possibly the most important and at the same time most neglected area in Christianity. Tim brings a fresh understanding along with practical ways in which we can develop this most vital relationship.

We (John G. Lake Ministries) are proud to have Tim as a part of our ministry. We look forward with anticipation for each new book Tim writes.

Curry R. Blake
General Overseer, John G. Lake Ministries
www.jglm.org

POTENTIALS AND PURPOSES OF SPIRIT LIFE

OUR PROMISED POSITION

In the Old Testament, the people of God were promised a place they could call home. It was a place where there was no lack, a place where they could grow and become the worldwide superpower. God prepared and provided prime real estate for an entire nation to be planted. Not only that, He gave them a kingdom structure and government that was flawless in how it could direct and grow this nation. Sadly, the people who were meant to take possession of this land did not have the consistent leadership and discipline to believe, apply, and possess all that God had promised for them. The potential this nation had was not fully realized.

Today, in the New Testament, we are in the same place these people were, except that our promised land is not physical property, but a position in the realm of the Spirit. This is shown in Second Peter 1:3-4:

> ...as His divine power has given to us all things that pertain to life and godliness, through the knowledge of Him who called us by glory and virtue, by which have been given to us exceedingly great and precious promises, that **through these you may be partakers of the divine nature**, having escaped the corruption that is in the world through lust.

The Israelites had a promised *land,* but we have been given a promised *nature.* What this is, is a position that God has for us where we can easily take a part of God's divine nature—His power, His glory, His virtue, His resources—and not get contaminated by any of the corruptions that lust wreaks on humankind.

JESUS WASN'T DONE YET

After Jesus rose from the dead, He knew His job was not completed until He could get His disciples into the same position that He had. His work on the cross finished preparing everything for humankind, but He still wanted us activated in everything He prepared for us.

> *...to whom He also presented Himself alive after His suffering by many infallible proofs, being seen by them during forty days and speaking of the things pertaining to the kingdom of God. And being assembled together with them, He **commanded them not to depart** from Jerusalem, but to **wait for** the Promise of the Father, "which," He said, "you have heard from Me...But you shall receive power when the Holy Spirit has come upon you; and you shall be witnesses to Me in Jerusalem, and in all Judea and Samaria, and to the end of the earth"* (Acts 1:3-4,8).

Jesus said this is our number one priority. We must not do *anything* until we get rooted into this place in the Spirit! Some people get the wrong ideas about this baptism in the Holy Spirit; some people think this is a one-time experience that is not really relevant for the rest of their Christian lives. In actuality, this is the doorway into the position in the Spirit that God has for us! If salvation is the door and faith turns the doorknob, then this *life* in the Spirit is the rest of the home *that God wants us to live in!* How sad it is that most people just stand in the doorway, looking at lives that others have lived in this home, both past and present, wishing they could someday, somehow be zapped into this place. Little do they know that this is available to *anyone who will choose to step inside.* Just like the home makeover shows, everyone cries and shouts for joy when they see the outside of their new home, but the question is, "Do you want to see *the rest of the house?*"

VICTORY IS IN YOUR FOCUS

Before we go any further, I want to remind us that this promised life in the Spirit is not a suggestion for us to think about; it is a command that we must obey! People wonder why sin, the flesh, the devil, and the world seem to have so much power and influence in this hour. It begins to cause many to doubt the power of the Gospel. They wonder— *Does it even work? Or does just staying a Christian have to be such a struggle all our days on Earth?* Some people are worse; they don't even ask these questions. They just give up and say, "Oh well, I know I'm going to Heaven. So if I have these weaknesses I can't overcome, God understands and still loves me."

However, Galatians 5:16 gives the simple key to victory: *"Walk in the Spirit and you shall not fulfill the lust of the flesh."* There is no victory unless we know *how to walk* in the Spirit. It's just like the saying about physical exercise—if you don't use it, you lose it! If you don't exercise your physical body, obesity, weakness, and sickness will eventually come in! It is simply the nature of the world and body we live in. So it is in the realm of the Spirit; we must *keep* moving in it to keep the corruption out.

Yet, the apostle Paul made it sound so simple! He didn't make it sound like this Christian life was such a struggle to overcome the lust of the flesh; he just said *"walk…and you will not fulfill the lust of the flesh."* This gives us a clue that this life is *not primarily* a fight against all the powers of the flesh against us, but it is simply a focus on letting the Spirit of God flow through our beings in every situation. When we do that, the lust of the flesh is automatically flushed out. What a great truth.

BE HONEST WITH YOURSELF

However, Paul said that this life must be *chosen*. When we flip on the light switch, the darkness is automatically flushed out, but we must still *choose* to turn it on! To answer those who would say, "Amen, Paul, that's what I am doing. I'm living in that light" (but really aren't)—he goes on to describe the dark works of the flesh: adultery, sexual immorality, impurity, lustfulness, idolatry, sorcery, hatred, loving to argue, selfish jealousy, outbursts of anger, selfish ambition, angry disagreements, false doctrines, envy, murder, drunkenness, rioting (see Gal. 5:19-21). This list describes a tormented life that is gripped by self-destruction. In contrast, Paul describes the life that the Spirit of God produces: love, joy, peace, endurance, kindness, goodness, faith, humility, self-control (see Gal. 5:22-23).

Which extreme do you live in? There is no neutral ground for long. Pressure always reveals who you are on the inside! How did you respond in the last challenge? The last temptation? The last time life disappointed you? The last time someone hurt you? Well, thank God for it because in that situation it was revealed what state you are in and what you are dealing with. Now, you must make the choice about where you *want* to be. Do you really want to live with this ticking time bomb of the flesh? Or do you want the victorious life flowing from the Spirit?

TRAINING FOR DESTINY

Life in the Spirit is the *only* way to victory in the Christian life. (Actually, it is not just the way to victory; it *is* the *continual* victory of the Christian life!) Not your church, not your friends, not your family, not your books, not your education, not your gifts, talents, self-image, hopes, or dreams—*none* of these are your way to victory, even though some of these may point you in the right direction. Hopefully this book can be one of those pointers. In the end, you will have to come back to the truth that Paul says so well in Romans 8:12-14:

> *Therefore, brethren, we are debtors—not to the flesh, to live according to the flesh. For if you live according to the flesh you will die; but if by the Spirit you put to death the deeds of the body, you will live. For as many as are led by the Spirit of God, these are sons of God.*

You will *never* win the battle against your flesh with tools invented by the flesh! The flesh desires are too deeply rooted in human nature. Only the Spirit of God knows how to go straight to the core of the problem, burn it out, and transform you into the child of God that He wants you to be. However, even though this is a simple solution, it will not be so easy to do! Yes, it will involve a change of habits, lifestyle, and perhaps—dare we say—how you define your present "personality."

Do not fear. What you see as your life now is just a dirty, dried-up seed. You may shrug that off with, "Well, my life is not *that* bad." But it's *only* when you bury it in the life of the Spirit that you will truly see the power, life, and beauty that God wants to bloom out of you. *What we are talking about is **not** some theoretical theological knowledge, but a very real daily experience of the Spirit in your life.* You and I are looking for tangible results. Even the world is looking for tangible results (see Rom. 8:19). Don't believe any lie from religion that tells you that God doesn't give tangible results anymore. Are you ready to begin your training?

INTRODUCTION REVIEW

1. What did the Israelites lack, causing them to not take full posses-
    sion of the Promised Land?

    "They did not have _____ and _____ to
    _____, _____, and _____ all that was
    promised for them."

2. Our promised land is not _____, but in the realm of
    the _____.

3. So we do have not a promised land, but a promised _____

4. What was Jesus' number one priority for His followers after
    His resurrection?

5. The baptism of the Holy Spirit is the doorway into the position in
    the Spirit that God has for us.

    Then salvation is the _____ and _____ turns
    the doorknob.

6. What is the meaning behind Galatians 5:16?

    _____

    _____

    _____

    _____

    _____

7. We   need   to   learn   how   to   _____ · _____
    _____ _____!

8. Our fight is not primarily a fight against all the powers of the flesh, but is a _____ on letting the Spirit of God flow through our being in every situation.

9. Paul said this life must be _____.

10. There is no _____ ground.

11. The only way to continual victory in the Christian is _____ _____ in the _____.

12. Explain the meaning of Romans 8:12-14.

    _____

    _____

    _____

    _____

    _____

13. You will never win the battle against your flesh with tools invented by the _____, but by the _____.

14. This must be a _____ experience.

PART I

SPIRIT, SOUL,
AND BODY

CHAPTER 1

A THREE-PART BEING

Now may the God of peace Himself sanctify you completely; and may your whole spirit, soul and body be preserved blameless at the coming of our Lord Jesus Christ. He who calls you is faithful, who also will do it (1 Thessalonians 5:23-24).

As we begin the training, we must understand that this verse gives us an important revelation of how we are made by God. This is *vitally* important. We know in Genesis that God made human beings a special creation—in His image and likeness. We are different from plants; plants have a body, but not a soul or spirit. We are different from animals; animals may have a body and a soul (mind, will, emotions), but not an eternal spirit.

Only humankind has a spirit. Humans were given a spiritual nature to commune with God like unlike any other creature. In fact, only humanity was given the ability to move into the realm of the spirit. That was meant to be as easy for people as breathing. This is how it was in the Garden of Eden with Adam and Eve. They related to God, a spiritual Being, (with their spirits) as easily as they related to each other (with their souls) and to the physical world around them (with their bodies). However, after they sinned, this spirit part of them was cut off from God's source of life.

KNOW THE RULES

The spiritual realm has rules and boundaries, just like this physical world has rules and boundaries. If someone jumps off a cliff and tries to violate the physical law of gravity, it can result in physical death. In the same way, when a spiritual law is violated, it results in spiritual death, which means that the ability to move in a healthy, free way in that spiritual realm is cut off.

It is important to know these laws (in both the spiritual and the natural) because there are laws that supersede other laws. For example, the law of lift in the physical realm is stronger than the law of gravity. This law of lift enables you to get into an airplane and go thousands of feet into the air, and yet come back down to the ground safely. In the realm of the spirit, mercy is stronger than the law of sin and death. This enables a person who has sinned against God and people to be released from the consequences of hell and perpetual spiritual failure.

It is important to know how to apply these principles and to know how they work together in their proper jurisdiction. *"For the law of the Spirit of life in Christ Jesus has made me free from the law of sin and death"* (Rom. 8:2). Just like the law of sin and death, there are laws and principles in the flesh and soul that have power to control you. Self-help books, psychologists, generational curses, and statistics on success and failure are very real to humankind. However, when you step into applying the higher law of the Spirit of life through your spirit, those lower laws no longer have the final say in your life! But to apply the higher law, you have to align yourself accordingly.

DIVINE ORDER

Now may the God of peace Himself sanctify you completely; and may your whole spirit, soul and body be preserved blameless at the coming of our Lord Jesus Christ. He who calls you is faithful, who also will do it (1 Thessalonians 5:23-24).

This passage gives a divine order for the restoration of humankind's three parts: spirit, soul, and body. The human spirit (and the spiritual realm in general) rules over the other two realms of the soul and the physical body. For this reason, and in light of how humankind was created, the proper, truthful definition of humanity, is this: A person *is* a spirit who *possesses* a soul and *lives in* a body. We do not just *have* spirits; we *are created as* eternal spirits. This is why we will live forever after our physical bodies die—either in Heaven or in hell. What makes people what they *really are* is their spirit nature. That is the core of every person. However, for the sake of defining each part, we will talk in terms of "having" a spirit, soul, and body.

Now, in applying this divine order of restoration of God's Kingdom design for our being, we must place the spirit as king, the soul as the servant, and the body as the slave. The spirit, as king, has complete authority to rule, direct, give executive commands, and have ownership over all the resources of the kingdom. The soul, as the servant, is to give information, make sure that the king has all the resources needed, and be an ambassador and a steward of supplies to other parts of the kingdom. The servant must represent the king well and understand and deliver messages properly. Finally, the body is the slave. A slave has no personal will, but must strictly carry out orders without question. The slave has desires, but makes the desires of the king the utmost priority. A slave has an extremely disciplined lifestyle and must be ready to jump into action at the slightest snap of the king's fingers.

MADE TO DOMINATE

Our spirits are king. In Revelation 1:5-6 and 5:9-10, the testimony of the redeemed is that Jesus Christ has made them kings on the earth. That is not talking about natural positions of president, king, prime minister, ruling the natural governments of the earth (primarily), but it is talking about humanity spiritually. The spirit dominates over the natural. When Jesus has made us kings in the spirit realm, that means we rule over the spiritual forces that rule over natural kings! This is another reason why Jesus is the King of kings! He is the King over the kingdom of kings, which is us now. Our kingly spirits submit to the Kingship of the Spirit of the Lord Jesus Christ.

"IT'S FINISHED"—SO WHAT DO WE DO?

The sad thing about religious Christianity is that First Thessalonians 5:23-24 is not taught or understood. Salvation is a complete work over the three parts of our beings. When Jesus cried out on the cross, He did not say "It is one-third finished." He said *"It is finished"* (John 19:30). Everything that humankind was cut off from in the Garden of Eden because of disobedience, was recovered by the obedient sacrifice of Jesus Christ. God can now have fully restored contact with all three parts of people, not just in the spiritual, but in the soul and body also.

To demonstrate that, at the same time that Jesus died on the cross, the veil in the Holy of Holies of the temple was torn in two from top to bottom. From "top to bottom" symbolizes that God Himself opened the way to come down, unlike many religions in which people are trying to get up to Him. The temple is a representation of our beings, also having three parts. The outer court represents our bodies, the inner court, or holy place, our souls, and the Holy of Holies our spirits.

All of the furniture in each of these places gives a great illustration of how God designed our being.

But right now the only thing I want to emphasize is where the breakthrough happened in the temple after Jesus died on the cross. It happened at the point between the Holy of Holies and the inner court. The Holy of Holies was previously cut off from everyone except for one priest, once a year. The manifest presence of God and people were separated from each other. But after *"It is finished,"* God took the initiative to move *out* of the Holy of Holies into the inner court and then into the outer court! What this means for us is that salvation is no longer just a hidden spiritual thing in our spirits, but can now be manifested in our souls and bodies also. It is *completely* finished.

When our spirits (through salvation) have contact with God, they are *holy*. When our souls have contact with God, they are *happy*. When our bodies have contact with God, they are *healthy*. Philippians 2:12-13 says that we must *"...work **out** [from our spirits our]...own salvation with fear and trembling; for it is God who works in you both to will [in our souls] and to do [with our bodies] for His good pleasure."* This Scripture commands us to take the presence of God out of the Holy of Holies (our spirits), bringing it into our souls so it can also manifest in our bodies. *That* is our work.

Our goal is to release our recreated spirits so we can truly live what Christianity was intended to be, a 100 percent supernatural life. Everything must align with the king—our spirits. It is like a combination lock. We do not try to dial the last number in first! We put in the first number, second number, third number—and the lock is opened! Once our spirits, souls, and bodies are aligned with God, nothing can stop Him from being all He wants to be through our lives. God will not invade Earth; He will stand at the door and knock. If we *know* the combination, we can let Him in, and that is the life that will change the world. This is because *now* the world can *see* Him. It is also the life that every human dreams of having. *"For the earnest expectation of the creation **eagerly** waits for the revealing of the sons of God"* (Rom. 8:19).

CHOOSING TO KEEP OUR SPIRITS UNLOCKED

This is the essence of this training—training ourselves to dial the combination to our spirits—*and keep it open!* It is not something that happens "by chance" or "in God's sovereign timing." How many of us have won the lottery lately? That happens by *chance*. But we all turned on the lights in our homes today. That happens by *choice*. God is not in the business of playing favorites. He is in the business of showing us the choice we all have to live His life in the Spirit. All of creation is waiting for us to *"Arise, shine; for your light has come! And the glory of the Lord is risen upon you"* (Isa. 60:1). The revealing is not God's choice—it is ours.

QUESTIONS TO CHALLENGE US

So the question is this: *Are we living from the inside out or still trying to live outside-in?* Sin corrupted the order of God. Now most people (even Christians) live with their bodies as king, their souls as the servant (to their bodies), and their spirits as the slave (to both). This is a complete tragedy and will surely lead to the destruction of the purpose and life of God in them. We *must* put each part back in the proper order so God can fulfill His promise to sanctify them *completely* for His use. Paul speaks about this very strongly in Romans 12:1-2:

> *I beseech you therefore, brethren, by the mercies of God* [powerful higher law in the realm of the spirit, that you must align with], *that you present your bodies* [as slaves] *a living sacrifice, holy, acceptable to God, which is your reasonable service* [the way your body is *designed* to live]. *And do not be conformed to*

this world [because the world pressures you to live outside-in], *but be transformed* [so you can live inside-out, releasing God's life from your kingly spirit to change everything] *by the renewing of your mind, that you may prove* [clearly show to everyone and tangibly experience] *what is that good and acceptable and perfect will of God.*

What an opportunity for a great life! However, all this understanding should provoke some more important questions. *How* do we release our spirits to rule our souls and bodies? *How* do we align our bodies and souls with our spirits? *How* do we really know what our bodies desire, our souls desire, and our spirits desire? *How* can our bodies be satisfied and healthy by being slaves? *How* can our souls actually be happy being servants? Are our spirits going to be silent kings; will we have to guess what our spirits want, feel, and say? And…is living this way really that important?

EXPANDING OUR POTENTIAL

This training book will answer these questions. Concerning the last question, as we close this chapter, let me inspire you. We are living in an age where technology is expanding exponentially. People's minds are expanding to extraordinary possibilities in communication, travel, health, military, entertainment, and much more. However, even as we are discovering these things, we can never forget this truth: *People's inventions can never improve on God's creation.* Everything people invent is already a possibility or already perfected in the realm of the spirit.

In communication, it is possible to perceive people's thoughts—Jesus did it (see Mark 2:8; Matt. 22:18); prophets such as Elisha did it (see 2 Kings 2:1-3; 5:25-26); the apostle Peter did it (see Acts 8:18-22). It is also possible to see events in the past, present, and future without television—many prophets and men and women of God did this. In travel it is possible to be translated from one place to another place many miles away without walking or using a car, airplane, or other vehicle; Philip did this (see Acts 8:38-40). In health, it is possible to be completely healed without the use of medicines or surgery and without any side effects; the examples in the Bible are too numerous to name. It is also possible to be so healthy that your body doesn't have the effects of aging; Moses and Caleb did this (see Deut. 34:7; Josh. 14:10-11). Militarily, it is possible to have legions of angels at our side, waiting for our orders to do whatever we ask to our enemies; Elisha did this, simply giving the command for every one of the enemy to be struck blind. Not one angel missed the target (see 2 Kings 6:16-18).

The possibilities of spirit life are endless. The Gospel of Jesus Christ comes with signs and wonders—it makes the natural world astonished and causes people to say, *"How did you do that?"* They look for natural reasons, but they will keep wondering because there is no natural explanation except, *"In Him we live, move, and have our being"* (Acts 17:28a). However, even with all these spectacular displays, the real reason that living a strong spirit life is so important is that it is the *only way* to truly be a success. It is the only way to truly please God and see His will done in our lives. If we want to successfully discover and accomplish our destinies, there is no other way than through this Spirit life (see Rom. 8).

"A THREE-PART BEING" REVIEW

1. Write out First Thessalonians 5:23-24.

2. What are the differences between people, plants, and animals?

    Plants have a _____, but not a soul or spirit.

    Animals may have a body and a soul, but not an _____

    _____.

    People have a _____ _____ to commune
    with God. Only people were given the ability to move into the
    realm of the spiritual.

3. What happened when Adam (humanity) sinned?

    We were _____ _____ from God's source of life.

4. When a spiritual law is _____, there is spiritual death,
    which means that the ability to move in a healthy free way in that
    spiritual realm is cut off. However, in both the spiritual and physi-
    cal realm, there are some laws that supersede other laws.

5. In the spiritual realm, _____ is stronger than the law of

    ___ _____ _____.

6. In the divine order a person *is* a _____ who *possesses* a
    _____ and *lives* in a _____.

7. In the restoration of this divine order, the spirit is _____, the
    soul is _____, and the body is _____.

8. What do Revelation 1:5-6 and 5:9-10 say we are? We are

    _____ ___ ____ _____.

9. We rule over the spiritual forces that rule over

   _____ _____!

10. _____ was recovered by the obedient sacrifice of Jesus.

11. Salvation is manifested in our spirits, but also can be in our

    _____ and _____.

12. Through salvation our spirits have contact with God and they
    are _____. Our souls have contact with God and they are
    _____. When our bodies have contact with God they
    are _____.

13. Our _____ is to bring God out of our spirits into our bodies
    and souls (see Phil. 2:12-13).

14. It is our _____ to live His life in the Spirit (see Rom. 8:19;
    Isa. 60:1). Are we living from the inside out or still trying to live
    outside-in?

15. Read Romans 12:1-2. What needs to happen to two parts of our be-
    ings for transformation to happen?

    _____

    _____

16. People's inventions can never _____ on God's
    _____ (us). If we want to successfully discover and ac-
    complish our destinies—there is no other way than through the
    spirit life.

17. Write out three examples of spirit life given on page 33.

    _____

    _____

CHAPTER 2

THE BODY—OUR EARTH SUIT

Since we have already reviewed the divine order of the three parts of humankind, let us examine each in greater detail to show their functions, desires, and potentials when they are aligned properly.

GOD LOVES OUR BODIES

We all have bodies. Everyone must acknowledge this fact about life on Earth. In space, we need space suits to survive in that environment; in the same way, on Earth we need "Earth suits" to function in this environment! Next, we must acknowledge that *God* gave us our bodies. He designed our bodies for everything we would need to do on this earth. Whether man, woman, child, black, red, white, tall, short, fat, skinny, blonde, brunette, green-eyed, brown-eyed, and so forth—He designed our bodies. God *loves* our bodies. This is why Jesus felt compassion and healed every sick and injured body He came into contact with. Say this out loud, *"God loves my body!"*

We don't have to be Miss Universe or on the cover of *GQ* magazine to be beautiful or handsome; all of our bodies are amazingly crafted (see Ps. 139:13-14). Any human anatomy textbook shows how miraculous we are; our DNA is so intricately designed. Just like we sing to God "there is none like You," He sings to us also, *"There is none like you—no* one else can touch My heart like *you* do." Of course, many of us may not fully realize this yet, but as we grow and learn about these things, we will find that this is so true. Our bodies are unique, special.

But our bodies will never *experience* this until we understand this next truth also: *God **wants** our bodies.* We may get nervous at that thought, but actually, this is the good part. *Our bodies were **designed** for the presence of God in a unique and powerful way.* Like a missing piece of a puzzle being found and put in place, like an electrical appliance whose plug has just found a socket—so is the presence of God to our physical bodies. They really come alive. Everything begins to function correctly, and the unique beauty of the Lord shines through us. Say this out loud—*"God **wants** my body!"*

In Acts 2:17 it says, *"And it shall come to pass in the last days, says God, that I will pour out of My Spirit on **all flesh**...."* God wants our bodies! It doesn't matter what our bodies look like; *He wants them.* Even for those of us who feel that there are flaws in our DNA for illness or deformity, the Bible declares that God has ordained a glorious healing to manifest how much He wants us to live life to the fullest (see John 9:1-3). Hebrews 10:5 states what God really wants from people—for us to offer Him the bodies that He gave us. This verse tells about Jesus' body being prepared for God's will: *"Therefore, when He came into this world, He said, 'Sacrifice and offering You did not desire, but a body You have prepared for Me.'"* Amazing—God wants the bodies that He gave to us!

SUPERNATURALLY TUNED

What can He do with our bodies? First of all, He will make them *supernatural.* What is commonly called "flowing in the anointing" is actually the process of mixing the human body with the power of the Holy Spirit. Every natural thing our bodies now do, in obedience to the Holy Spirit working with our spirits, causes supernatural effects. By themselves, our bodies' five senses are normal information-gatherers. But when the anointing moves through them, they begin to know things that they would not naturally know!

By looking at other people, we can tell what kind of people they are. We begin to see the reality beneath the surface. We see what kind of spirits they have, and what their real needs are. We start to see the right path to go when we are lost. We see things before they happen. We begin to hear things in people's voices that help us discern deception or faith or pain or even their thoughts. We begin to taste or smell when certain kinds of spiritual characteristics are near—greed, holiness, homosexuality, uncleanness, worship, and more. Even in the natural, the senses of taste and smell work together.

We also begin to feel and touch in a supernatural way. John G. Lake and others I know of testified that they were able to lay their hands upon sick people and, because their bodies had become so spiritually sensitized, they were able to know the exact location of the sickness and to what degree the disease was progressing. How is that for a quick diagnosis? Some also have their physical bodies tuned to sense and then distinguish God's presence from an angelic or demonic presence.

BRINGING HEAVEN INTO THE EARTH

Now, to many people, this may seem very spooky and strange, but this is truly the way God originally designed our bodies to be—tools to bring the supernatural into the natural. Jesus taught us to pray that God's Kingdom would come and His will would be done *on Earth* as it is in Heaven (see Matt. 6:10). Our bodies are created from the dust of the earth. Just like our wills respond to what we sense, so God's will must respond to what He senses through us! If our nervous systems shut down, our wills are directionless and useless. God wants to mix His Spirit's nervous system with our nervous systems to make them respond not just to our wills, but to respond now to His will in the Spirit. God can use whatever He wants for His glorification, and He chose to purchase our bodies so they could supernaturally glorify Him.

> Or do you not know that your body is the temple of the Holy Spirit who is in you, whom you have from God, and you are not your own? For you were bought at a price; therefore **glorify God in your body** and in your spirit, which are God's (1 Corinthians 6:19-20).

We should believe that God can use our bodies in this way just like God used Jesus' body for these things on Earth.

DESIRES OF THE BODY

So we see that when the body is plugged into the spirit, the physical body becomes a supernatural conduit of God's power and presence. This is the purpose and potential of God for our bodies, and this should be our pursuit. However, the body is a strange creature. It has wants and desires of its own that are *not* rooted in the realm of the spirit, but in itself. These fleshly desires of people become the bait of satan to trap the nations of the earth.

Our bodies want three basic things: food, sex, and comfort. Our bodies scream for these things from the time we are born until the time we die (except for the sexual desire, which only awakens during a certain time in life—definitely not when we are babies). These desires are *strong* and can be raging and overpowering at times, if we let them be that way. God actually created them to be strong. They are a part of living and surviving on Earth. God created them to each have their place in life.

If we did not have these desires, we would not want to live on Earth. We would actually destroy ourselves and die. We wouldn't want to eat or drink and so would suffer malnutrition and die. If a doctor sees someone (especially a baby) who has no desire to eat or drink, that is a serious problem! If we didn't want any kind of comfort, we would end up abusing our bodies and ending our lives early because we would violate physical laws that require rest, proper posture, taking care of the body, and so forth. Finally, if we never wanted sex, the human race would hardly ever procreate—knowing the responsibility of a marriage and child raising. The death rate would overwhelm the birth rate, and each proceeding generation would have a greater burden of taking care of the Earth than the previous one.

PUTTING THE BODY IN ITS PLACE

So these desires are necessary. But they must be fulfilled with extreme accuracy! Say this: *"My body does not know how to live."* It only has desires. It does not have inherent wisdom for living. Our bodies will try to use these desires to pull our souls and spirits out of control and (because of these raging desires) try to become kings when they were only meant to be slaves. The body has no conscience. It does not see a wedding ring to avoid the consequences of adultery. It does not see the heart attack that comes from a lifetime of eating hamburgers. It does not see the lung cancer that comes from smoking cigarettes all day. Our bodies' desires cause them to become stupid when they take control. Our bodies satisfy all their desires and then wonder why these bad effects happen: *Why is this enraged husband shooting a gun at me? It was only sex. Why is my heart hurting, and this pain shooting down my arm? I think I need another hamburger and a beer. Why* (cough, cough) *can't I* (wheeze, pant) *climb up my* (gasp) *stairs of my house? And where* (cough, cough) *is my pack of cigarettes* (gasp)? *Pray? What a waste of air. Especially when sleeping would feel so good right now...(yawn) yesss... problems leave when I sleep...peace and success can wait...Heaven can wait...zzzzz...*

Our bodies do not know how to live. If we allow our bodies' desires to have the first consideration in everything (or even most things) we do, our bodies' desires will grow out of control. Our bodies will eventually destroy themselves, as well as our souls and our spirits. God loves our bodies, and God promises in First Corinthians 3:17, *"If anyone defiles [destroys] the temple of God, God will destroy him. For the temple of God is holy [designed for God's special purpose], which temple you are."* We must know our bodies' place in God's designed order. If we do not diligently and carefully control our bodies' desires according to God's design, we *will* come into God's (and life's) judgment. On the other hand, if we fulfill them according to God's design, we will be greatly blessed with no regrets.

GOD NEEDS OUR BODIES TO BE STRONG

So what are our responsibilities concerning our bodies? Our responsibilities are simple—*care for* and *command* our bodies. As was already mentioned, the body is referred to as the *temple* of the Holy Spirit. In the Old Testament model of the temple, there was actually a tribe whose full-time job was to keep the temple *clean* and *in order*! This was not just to keep it shiny and beautiful, but so it would perform its *function effectively*! God is a holy God, and He required His temple to be holy so He could move through it. Thus we keep our bodies clean and in order not just to look beautiful or handsome, but so that God can function through them without hindrance.

Though it is said that *"man looks at the outward appearance, but the Lord looks at the heart"* (1 Sam. 16:7), this doesn't mean that the outward appearance doesn't matter to God! It does! The facts are, if we never get exercise, don't eat healthy foods, and are constantly physically exhausted, *it is next to impossible for us to become spiritually strong.* God needs our bodies to be strong in order to *obey Him.* Otherwise, we can't pray long, wake up (and stay awake!), praise God properly, minister for Him, have strength to endure, and so forth. Romans 12:1 says:

> *I beseech you therefore, brethren, by the mercies of God, to present your bodies a living sacrifice, holy, acceptable to God, which is your reasonable service.*

We must present our bodies as *living* sacrifices, not half-dead ones. This means we must be *healthy* because, in the Old Testament, every sacrifice must be strong and healthy. To offer a blemished, sickly animal was an abomination. They were disqualified from God's service. Even though this sounds harsh, we must truly get a revelation of how this *is* the model in the Word of God and also of how much God truly wants this for us. Jesus did not compromise or have pity upon anyone who was sickly or weak. He *healed* them and made them strong. This clearly shows what is God's will for every human body. Human bodies must be healthy and strong in order to obey Him! We can't have lazy bodies and obey God. After these people were healed, many used their newfound health to follow Him. If Jesus was our example, we must remember that He was always *on the move.* People had to have some kind of cardiovascular fitness just to keep up with Him!

MAKING OUR BODIES OBEY

The second responsibility is to *command* our bodies to obey God. The flesh does not naturally *want* to obey; we must *train* it to obey. If we think God will always give us instructions that are easy on our fleshly desires, we better think again. There *will* be times when the two will be in direct conflict. There will be times when we are tired, feeling weak, have to give up something our flesh likes, sleep places that we don't want to, wake up at times we don't want to, eat things we don't want to, refuse foods that we really want, give up habits that are physically relaxing for us at times, and so forth. No, God is not trying to be cruel, but our bodies are not kings! They are slaves and must be taught to put our spirits' pleasure first—*in an instant.*

Luke 16:11 says that if we are not faithful in natural things (like our natural bodies), God will not trust us with true riches (like the life of the Spirit). If we cannot take authority over the things of our bodies, there is no way we will be able to have the responsibility to have authority over the greater powers of the Spirit. *I cannot say that strongly enough.* This is why the first temptation Jesus had to overcome in the wilderness was concerning the desires of the flesh (see Luke 4:3-4). He had to pass the test of being responsible to say *no* to His flesh when His flesh was under tremendous pressure to yield to temptation.

Have you ever actually told your body a verbal "no"? Many people have not. They think that it is strange to talk out loud to their bodies. However, the more we go through this training, the more we will see that the voice is a primary tool of the spirit to be able to take control of and train the three parts of our beings.

PRACTICAL TRAINING TIPS FOR THE BODY

Our training for our bodies is how we train slaves. Their desires and wants must be able to be controlled and shut down at a moment's notice—with no complaints! This is our first goal in training our bodies.

1. *Your No Must Stand Strong*

First, find out what physical desire your body likes to do or doesn't like to do. For example, do you like to eat a certain kind of food? Would you go out of your way to be able to find and eat it?

How often? Is it daily? Weekly? Or just simply regularly? Take the opportunity for the next month to say "no" to your body concerning that food. (I'm talking specifically concerning any comfort food or junk food that your body craves; if you are eating some health food because of health reasons or a doctor's order, that is not something you should cut out.) When the opportunity presents itself to eat that food, tell your body "no" and watch the reaction! Slap your hand away, and tell your growling stomach "not today!" If your body reacts harshly to you, you have a lot of work ahead of you to train it. But if your body just quiets down and gives you an obedient "OK," you are making progress.

You will also feel the inward shift of strength go to your spirit. It is also interesting to see the reactions of people around you—who are also addicted to this certain kind of food—when *you* refuse it. They will react quite strongly. Sometimes they will even get angry. "What is wrong with you? Go ahead; eat it!" You will find out how seriously people take their food. One time God told me, *"The devil considers every act of personal discipline as an act of war against him."* So don't worry about other people's reactions. Smile, be polite, and change the focus of the conversation. You don't always have to explain what you are trying to do because they probably won't understand.

2. Wake It Up; Shut It Down

Next, does your body love to sleep? Train your body to wake up at a moment's notice and become fully awake and alert. Tell it, "Body, wake up *now* and be wide awake!" Don't let your body lie to you and say, "I need to sleep more; this is not fair; you are breaking the laws of nature by waking me up like this." *Your body can be trained to obey your spirit.*

> But if the Spirit of Him who raised Jesus from the dead dwells
> in you, He who raised Christ from the dead will also give life

to your mortal bodies through His Spirit who dwells in you (Romans 8:11).

Or as the saying goes, *"the Spirit who raised Jesus from the dead can get you out of bed!"* On the other hand, can you tell your body to sleep whenever you want to? If it is late at night, your body may say, "I'm not tired! I don't need to sleep. Let's eat ice cream and snacks; let's watch television." Tell your body, "Body, it is time to sleep. Shut down and restore yourself." Don't let your body rule you; you decide when it is time to wake up and sleep.

I have a friend who used to train himself militarily for terrorist activities before God radically saved him many years ago. He trained himself to not feel pain—to be able to go through harsh conditions without any complaining to be able to finish his mission. He even trained himself to sleep no matter what noise was around him and to be able to wake up in a moment's notice. After he was born-again, the personal discipline he had developed proved to be a valuable asset to his spiritual growth! Things of God came faster to him because of this capacity to make his body obey without complaining.

3. *Strategize to Be Healthy, Wealthy, and Wise*

Next, you need to make a schedule for proper eating, sleeping, and exercise. This is the hard part because it requires a permanent habit and lifestyle change. It *will* cost time and money. First of all, find out the things you *cannot* change. See if your work schedule is an immovable variable in your life. If you have to be at work at 9 A.M., you find out what you need to do to be there on time and that becomes your fixed variable. What time do you get off work? Let that also be as immovable as possible. Next, decide upon how many hours of sleep you need to be refreshed. For most people, it is between seven and eight hours a night. If you have a 50-hour work week (including travel and lunch time), you have another six hours each day (Monday through Friday). You have to make time to pray, eat, study, exercise, spend time with family and good friends, and take care of personal responsibilities (showering, shopping, answering mail, paying bills, cleaning, and so forth).

Make out a schedule for things you consider "vital, immovable priorities." These should be things like prayer, study, and eating. Make a time schedule for these. How much alone time do you want to pray—20 minutes, one hour? Set a time either in the morning or at night for this. (I recommend spending at least 10 minutes, no matter what, in the morning for prayer in order to start your day honoring the presence of God.) Do the same with your studying and eating (including preparation time). Time with family will also be a vital priority, but may not be fixed, depending on their activities and your ability to meet with them. *Make* time to talk with your spouse and *make* time to talk and play with your children as much as possible. You *will* make time for things that are really important to you.

Next, make a schedule for exercise. Where will you exercise? A nearby gym? Figure in your travel time. This would be more ideal if you are a person who needs motivation to work out. A home gym? This is more convenient, but has less variety of exercises, and more self-discipline is required. What are your fitness goals? Strength increase? Cardiovascular endurance? Maybe a mix of both? You will need 20-30 minutes for a basic aerobic workout and at least 30-40 minutes for a good strength workout with weights. Find out how long each workout will be and what focus each workout will be. (Here is an example. Monday, Wednesday, and Friday: aerobic stair-climbing, 20 minutes; chest, shoulders, and arms workout, 30 minutes. Tuesday and Thursday: back, legs, and abs workout, 40 minutes). Figure in the time for traveling and showering and put that on your schedule.

Now you can fix a time for sleep. What time will you sleep? Tell your body to shut down and sleep' at that time. What time will you wake up? Tell your body to wake up fully at that time.

THE POINT: DISCIPLINE YOUR DAY

Of course you may say, "It's not that easy; my life cannot be organized so neatly." I will tell you this: You must control your life as much as possible. (No, God will not control your life for you; for more on this, see the section on the will.) If you do not, it will be difficult to obey God because you are constantly being controlled by everything else but Him—your flesh, your friends, your relatives, your work, and so forth. You must decide who your Master is and serve Him only. Your flesh will be the major factor as it will try to buck any attempts to control it with a schedule that puts your spirit first and the flesh and soul in line. Eventually it will be trained, and everyone else will eventually respect the discipline you put into your life. An added benefit is this: Disorderly people will also eventually leave your life! Thank God for that!

Having said all this, there *will* be times and seasons when changes will have to be made in your schedule to accommodate something that is important to God and you, but you will have to get back to this life-giving routine as soon as you can. As much as possible, only keep your weekends free for special events and projects that you want to do. Never neglect the vitals for life on your weekend—such as prayer and study and sleep. The other things such as exercise, eating, family time, and such should be scheduled as much as possible, but these can be more flexible for the sake of others (but not nonexistent) on weekends. Learn more about healthy eating, taking vitamins, and developing a quality exercise plan. These are quality investments for your life. Your body is not as important as the next two areas we will discuss—the soul and spirit—but it is nonetheless important to God and His destiny for you. As you grow in understanding of time management and taking care of your body, you will learn the most effective strategies for becoming healthy, wealthy, and wise (see 3 John 2).

WINNER TAKES ALL

Even though our bodies are not as important as our souls and spirits, learning to discipline the flesh is the hardest battle of spirit life training. *It may be only one third of your being, but that doesn't mean that it is 33 percent of the fight!* Percentage-wise, I feel that it would be closer to 60 percent. I know that once victory over the flesh is experienced, victory in the soul and spirit are much easier. Jesus declares this in Luke 9:23-24:

> *If anyone desires to come after Me, let him deny himself, and take up his cross daily, and follow Me. For whoever desires to save his life will lose it, but whoever loses his life for My sake will save it.*

It is a paradox, but when we die to our fleshly desires, we destroy our number one enemy to spirit life. Yes, the spiritual truth is that there are three enemies to our lives—the world, the flesh, and the devil. But which is the most important enemy to fight first? *The flesh.* Once we destroy the power of the flesh, we destroy the power of the world to influence us. How can we influence a dead person? Once we destroy the power of the flesh, we destroy the power of the devil to tempt us to use our five senses to fulfill the lust of the flesh. Immediately the devil's key weapons are stripped. The serpent in the Garden of Eden was cursed to only eat the dust of the ground. Our flesh is made of the dust of the ground. Once we cut off the devil's food supply, it's like we are choking him to death.

NO MATTER RICH OR POOR

No matter whether we are riding high in the fullness of prosperity or struggling to keep our heads above water in the midst of poverty, *no one* is exempted from the need to discipline the flesh. I mean *no one.* Neither the pain of poverty nor the privilege of prosperity should give us a sense of entitlement to lessen our discipline on the desires of the flesh. When our flesh insists, "I work hard. Life is tough sometimes. *I deserve this,*" we must remember that our flesh must *never* be promoted beyond the position of a slave. We must never give it the position to negotiate to have its way!

UNDERSTAND THIS DANGER

I find it dangerous today how people will believe and pursue God for prosperity and then use that prosperity as a means to an end of empowering their fleshly pleasures. This is so backwards and will surely lead to spiritual poverty and destruction. Prosperity can give us great power to bless and do good, *but the greatest prosperity is the potential found in a strong spirit.* Never forget that. No matter what our present economic status is, it is truly the strength of our spirits that can take us up or drag us down. So if we can use prosperity, comforts, and modern conveniences to untangle the natural affairs of life and to discipline the flesh in a more effective manner—that is true prosperity! But if these comforts and conveniences lead to further entanglements and weights, it is better to cut them off than to miss out on the power of this spirit life.

This is what Jesus was talking about in Matthew 18:8-9. God does not get pleasure in the amputation of what He created as good (hands, feet, eyes, or the modern technologies we create to help us), but if we can't use something to produce more spirit life, it is *more profitable* to get rid of it. We must ask ourselves, *What are they producing?* With all the time we are saving with our technologies and speed of communication, we should have freed up our lives so significantly to worship, pray, serve, and work with

God so much more; to pursue God so much more; to tap so much deeper into the realms of the Spirit. But is that truly what we see happening?

I would suggest that often we pursue time-saving conveniences and forget the purpose for which we are saving time. I am not against these things at all; the point is that we often use them to empower our flesh rather than our spirits. We understand the need to cut off something negative like cancer in order to save life, but to cut off something that seems perfectly good seems insane—*unless what you can gain from its loss is so excellent that even something good will appear repulsive and detrimental.* This points to the potential riches that can be tapped into in this life of the spirit; whatever we let go of will never be greater than what can be tapped into inside of our spirits. *"You will show me the path of life; in Your presence is fullness of joy; at Your right hand are pleasures forevermore"* (Ps. 16:11). No matter how good technology gets, nothing beats what we already possess! Let's pray to see it now.

Father, I pray the eyes of our understanding would be enlightened by Your Spirit of Wisdom and Understanding, that we would know the hope of Your calling for us, that we would know the riches of Your glorious inheritance inside of us, and that we would know what is the exceeding greatness of Your power in and through us who believe. Father, we need to **see** *the potential of this awesome gift of life in the spirit that You have given us! And yes, as we see it, we will clearly know that nothing on Earth will distract us from living in it!*

Once we can see it clearly, our choices in the midst of prosperity (as well as poverty) will become much simpler.

"SUCH AS I HAVE, I GIVE UNTO YOU"

After our bodies are well trained, they can be sensitive to the sensations of the spirit. Our bodies will be seamless conduits whereby they will both pick up spiritual information and release the spirit. When our bodies are submitted and aligned to the soul and spirit by discipline to the Word of God, this can become simply a choice. We can choose to pick up what is going on spiritually in our environment, focus, and release power and life from our spirits to meet the case. No matter if that need is healing, deliverance, discernment, joy, or conviction, our spirits make the decision to release what we have and our bodies freely release it into the situation.

> Then Peter said, "Silver and gold I do not have, but what I do have I give you: In the name of Jesus Christ of Nazareth, rise up and walk." And he took him by the right hand and lifted him up, and immediately his feet and ankle bones received strength (Acts 3:6-7).

God designed our bodies for spiritual service to express the glory of God. Let's expect them to work in that capacity effectively. We must discipline them and start training and using them for these purposes right away. Practice, practice, practice....

"THE BODY—OUR EARTH SUIT" REVIEW

1. God gave us our _____. God _____ our bodies! Our bodies were _____ for the presence of God in a unique and powerful way!

2. Read Acts 2:17 and Hebrews 10:5. How does God see the body?

3. What some call the _____ is the process of mixing the human body with the power of the Holy Spirit.

4. Our five senses are information-gatherers. Using the power of the Holy Spirit, we can: _____ things that we wouldn't naturally know; see things in the _____, smell and _____ things in the spirit realm. We can begin to sense and _____ things in a supernatural way like John G. Lake and others. Some can have their _____ so tuned they can physically sense and then distinguish God's presence from an angelic or demonic presence.

5. Read First Corinthians 6:19-20. God wants to use our bodies just like He used _____ body on earth!

6. When the body is plugged into the _____, it becomes a supernatural _____ of God.

7. Our bodies desire three things. *Are these wrong or right?*

8. Say out loud: "My body does not know how to _____!" Our bodies only have desires, and if we allow those to have first consideration, they can grow out of control and will eventually destroy our bodies as well as your _____ and _____. Write out First Corinthians 3:17.

9. If we fulfill our bodies' desires according to God's design, we will be _____.

10. Our first responsibilities for our bodies are to _____ _____ and _____ them. God needs our bodies to be strong in order to *obey* Him.

11. Romans 12:1 says God wants a _____ sacrifice, not a _____-_____ one.

12. We must _____ our bodies to obey our commands to it. Remember our bodies are not _____, but our spirits are. What was the first temptation for Jesus in the wilderness?

13. The _____ is the main tool of our spirits to take control of the body, which is our main goal.

14. The _____ considers every act of personal discipline as an act of _____ against him.

15. Identify some of the strategies listed to be healthy, wealthy, and wise.

16. What is _____ to you, you *will* make time for. Learning to discipline the flesh may not be the most important element of spirit life training, but it is the hardest initial _____ of the training! Read Luke 9:23-24. Are there any shortcuts past these verses?

17. Our greatest prosperity is the _____ found in a strong spirit.

18. Read Psalm 16:11. How does this relate to what we just read in Luke 9:23-24 and what was discussed in the chapter?

19. First meditate upon and then pray the prayer found on page 51.

20. For this first phase of the training, find activities, including the ones listed below, in which to discipline your body.

    Food: Be able to record three instances in which you were able to tell your body "no" simply for the sake of not letting your body get its way. (See pages 44-47 for more details.)

    1) _____

    2) _____

    3) _____

    Be able to go to sleep and wake up on command.

    Start an exercise program. Organize your schedule to begin something this week.

    What exercises will you do?

    What days of the week will you do those exercises?

    How long will you exercise for?

    What goals do you have in your exercising?

21. Pray and ask God what other areas to discipline your body in that are specific to your situation. Note any addictions, unproductive fleshly habits, or creature comforts that limit you from obeying God. Also, note any sicknesses or pains that seek to keep your body from its full potential. Use your God-given authority to remind your body that it will do what your spirit wants it to, that your body is a happy, obedient slave. Care for it and yet specifically command what you want it to do. If your body rebels against your wishes, keep using your authority until it obeys God peacefully. Record three victories in any prayer journal you might have. We also always appreciate getting testimonies at spiritlifetraining@gmail.com.

CHAPTER 3

THE SOUL—THE LAST BATTLEGROUND

Over the course of the next six chapters, we will examine the many functions of the soul in our daily lives and in the life of one of the best-known Bible characters and contributors—David. But before we delve into the details, let's establish an overview of the soul in the context of the spiritual life.

From the beginning, the soul has been the portal through which the devil has entered humankind to tempt the flesh. It is fertile ground for such activity because so much of life plays out there. In fact, the soul is made up of five basic areas: emotion, intellect/reasoning, memory, imagination, and the will. That is a lot of territory—and the very place where the devil tries to blind humankind from understanding the Gospel of salvation (see 2 Cor. 4:3-4). It is where the devil tries to plant his strongholds against God's truth (see 2 Cor. 10:3-6). This area is so vital that, until we possess this part of our beings, we cannot possess anything else. *"By your patience possess your souls"* (Luke 21:19).

> *For what profit is it to a man if he gains the whole world and loses his own soul? Or what will a man give in exchange for his soul?* (Matthew 16:26)

Disciplining our bodies is the first major fight, but the soul is where the deciding bout is fought for control over the human spirit. If our souls are completely surrendered to God, there is no limitation for God moving through our bodies and spirits. This is a place of peace, prosperity, and power in our lives. *When we possess our souls and surrender them totally to God's work in our spirits, there is no stopping us.*

This is like the life of Jesus. He was completely poised in life. He had the strength to have peace in the midst of mobs, or to sleep in the midst of a storm. He never had a problem with doubt or worry; never failed in anything He did; was never shaken by any person's words, threats, or actions; and never had a time where needs confronted Him and fear gripped His mind. No one could manipulate Him. No one could take His joy. No one could frustrate Him. He had a life that no one else could take from Him.

People who have total control over their souls have a power that few have ever attained. Even when Jesus was tempted for 40 days, He could not be physically harmed in any way by the devil. The reason for this was that not one of the devil's temptations could take any ground inside Jesus' soul.

If we are willing to work hard to discipline both our souls and bodies, the enemy will not find any entrance into any part of our lives, either. Like I said, this is a power that very few have attained. However, before people start to think that this involves yoga or some Eastern New-Age meditation techniques, we need to understand that Jesus used none of these. He trained His soul the same way we can train ours—through aligning each part of our souls completely with the Word of God. Let's get started.

CHAPTER 4

EMOTIONS

Our emotions are identified as the "biggest" part of our souls. This is not because they are the most developed or even the strongest part of the soul, but it is because they are the most vocal part of the human soul! They have an ability to override the rest of the elements of our souls in a way that can be spectacular to watch.

OUR FUEL FOR ACTION

When our emotions are used in a godly way, they will express how God feels about something. *God has emotions!* He has feelings of joy, sorrow, peace, anger, urgency, jealousy, compassion, and more. When they are released in us in a proper way, perfectly aligned with God's thoughts and feelings, our emotions can be incredibly effective. They can be a powerful catalyst for a move of God. When Jesus released His emotions, they affected people in a powerful way. When He was at Lazarus' grave, he began to weep in intercession; this released the love of God in a powerful way and, even in the midst of unbelief, a man was raised from the dead (see John 11).

When Jesus went to the temple and saw the money-changers cheating the people and defiling the temple, the anger of God rose up in Him and provoked Him to action. He was not out of control with His anger as He carefully made a whip and then began to effectively clean house and chase these people out of the temple (see John 2:13-17). Emotions were His tool to do the will of God effectively. When the disciples came back full of wonder about their success in casting out demons, Jesus began to rejoice. He wanted to show them that the Father has great delight in revealing to them the power of His Kingdom (see Luke 10:17-21). The Bible is full of stories of how people used emotions for God's glory.

STOP THE ROLLERCOASTER

However, it is far more common to see emotions used in an ungodly way. Ungodly emotions will control us. They will put us on a rollercoaster of instability in life. One moment we are up, so happy with life. The next moment, we feel our lives are crashing around us, and we feel like committing suicide! Emotions will try to force us to live by their dictates, and they will try to possess our mouths and wills. *"I do what I feel like doing.* If I don't feel like doing it, I won't!" This is the rising python in our generation that is destroying the bonds of commitment in all areas of life. "As long as I feel good, I will stay here." If our employment is no longer "fun" for us, immediately we start doing a poor job and start looking for "a better opportunity." In relationships, if there is an emotional hurt or there is no longer the thrill of excitement, discovery, or romance, commitment is broken and immediately we start looking for a more entertaining or more emotionally comforting option.

THE WORLD'S PUPPET MASTER

This is creating a rising dictator in the world called "entertainment"—controlling the joysticks of our emotions. This emotional addiction of highs and lows is becoming an even more powerful addiction than any drug! "Make me laugh, make me cry, stimulate my emotions please!" Look at the price that people worldwide will pay and plan for entertainment and you will see the power that people have allowed emotions to have over them. It doesn't matter what part of the world people come from or how highly intelligent they are; the ruling force behind most people's lives is an addiction to emotional feelings. Some people who recognize this have actually learned to use their emotions as their most powerful weapon. They can use them to manipulate others through their self-pity, anger, lust, intimidation, and so forth. Emotions can be used to create a whole fantasy world, shockingly similar to what a drug can do.

Like Goliath intimidating the whole army of Israel, so emotional control will seek to bind us to a false sense of reality of who we are and what we can do. *And* once ungodly emotions rise up to speak through our mouths, that's it. We are finished. We have just cursed our lives with all kinds of pain. Relationships will be damaged; we could be fired from our jobs; we could be in all kinds of legal trouble; time, money, and energy are needlessly wasted; and the list goes on. We could end up spending years trying to repair the damage that our ungodly emotions just did in only a few moments through our mouths.

STOPPING EMOTIONAL DECEPTION IN ITS TRACKS

The first key to controlling our emotions is to doubt them. We cannot let them trick us into a false sense of reality. This is because what we "feel" may not be *real*. This is the first part of our souls that we must learn to control.

It is amazing to me how many times in the Bible God had to tell people, "Do not fear," before He could say *anything* else to them (see Gen. 15:1; Josh. 8:1; Isa. 37:5-7; Luke 1:30; Luke 2:10; Luke 5:10; Rev. 1:17).

Until they could put their emotions under control, God could not have any entrance into their lives. That is because, instead of living in the reality He was about to speak to them, they would live in the fantasy world that fear was chaining them into. What they had learned to "feel" was not *real*. People feel rejection when God has *not* rejected them. People feel like failures when God has *not* stopped giving them a hope and a future. People feel forced into a decision by despair and worry when God knows that if they will hold on to His Word a bit longer, the victory is just around the corner.

God's Word is reality. *Emotions, without the Word of God to give them substance, become horrible decision-makers.* That should be memorized. Imagine if we made all our decisions based on feelings of fear, anger, rejection, depression, lust, and so forth. What a life destined for destruction. Not long after the first sin, the first murder was committed by an emotionally dominated Cain (see Gen. 4:4-15). Because his negative emotions ruled his actions, his cursed life became a warning to anyone else who would follow his emotional example. *"Make no friendship with an angry man, and with a furious man do not go, lest you learn his ways and set a snare for your soul"* (Prov. 22:24-25).

BREAK THE CHAINS; GRAB THE REINS

So what do we do after we learn to doubt our emotions? We must begin to actually *control* them. Yes, this is possible. When we change our focus, we will change our feelings—every time. The longer we focus on a negative event, the more it will begin to warp our minds and emotions. When we choose to focus on something positive, our emotions will automatically begin to switch direction as well. Amazing. It is like a bit in the mouth of a stallion. Such a small device can control such a powerful beast.

In Psalm 42:5, David gives an example of talking to and directing his emotions: *"Why are you cast down, O my soul? And why are you disquieted within me? Hope in God, for I shall yet praise Him for the help of His countenance."* Even though the situation looked desperate, David commanded his emotions to hope in God! This training of his emotional control is documented abundantly in the Book of Psalms. He learned time and time again to encourage himself in God and His Word. Sometimes his life depended on it (see 1 Sam. 30:1-8).

The apostle Paul wrote the Book of Philippians from the filth of a first-century prison and while facing a possible death sentence; but again and again he wrote in that book, *"Rejoice in the Lord always. Again I will say, rejoice"* (Phil. 4:4). This also was a man who learned the power of proper emotional control.

Most successful characters in the Bible had to learn this skill. Emotions are powerful, but like military weapons, they must be fired in the right direction. We must grab hold of them so strongly! This is done through our boldly spoken words. "Emotions, you listen to me now! You will never control me. I control you by the Word and the Spirit of God!" "I *will* rejoice!" "I *will* love God and others!" "I *will* hate sin!" "I *will not* fear!" "I *will* hope!"

When we begin to declare these confessions with authority, our emotions learn to do what *we* want them to do, not what they are manipulated to do by circumstances, other people, or even the devil.

TEACHING OURSELVES WHAT TO FEEL

We will *not* feel like doing that when our emotions are raging in an opposite direction, but that is *precisely when we **must** do it*. That is a part of our training. We must tell ourselves again, "Listen emotions, what you *feel* is *not real*. What the Word of God says is real!" The Bible even talks about telling ourselves how to feel after we are corrected because of the human soul's tendency to feel rejected and hurt. The Bible says to actually *tell our souls to feel* **accepted** *and* **loved**, and to even *enjoy the correction* because *the reality is that it is for our highest good* (see Heb. 12:5-11; Prov. 9:8).

So when we feel our emotional temperature rising, that's the prime time for training our emotions. We must learn to *expect* this and remember to push our emotions into obedience through our forceful confession. So when something negative happens—that's great, not because it happened, but because we get a chance to work out our "I *will* rejoice!" confession; *we have to do this when it's hardest to do.* When we don't feel like loving God or when we feel apathetic toward people, that's fantastic! It's an opportunity to rise up on the inside, to smile and shout, "I *will* love God and others! I *love* God with *all* my heart! I *love* so-and-so!" As we verbally expand on these things, we will deliberately push our emotions to feel the right way.

This also opens a pathway for corresponding actions based on those words. Our emotions *will* eventually change! But we must take full advantage of these negative emotional moments for training purposes.

DON'T "GO WITH THE FLOW"—CHANNEL THE RIVER

There will be times when we must use our emotions to comfort and serve others (see Rom. 12:15). However, our emotions are not always meant to go with the flow of circumstances, *but they are primarily to give life and expression to our faith in God's character and His Word!* So, let's begin to care when no one cared for us. Let's choose to have compassion for those who have despitefully used us. Let's throw our heads back and laugh when the situation looks desperate. Say, "Ha ha ha," over and over again until the joy of the Lord begins to bubble up into a confession of victory with a dance to go along with it. It works!

Some may say, "But that doesn't change anything about my situation." If we try it, we will be surprised. The saying is that "our attitude determines our altitude in life," and no successful person would argue with that. True, attitude is just the beginning, but until we begin to control our emotions positively, we have already sabotaged ourselves from any chance of success. Successful people and opportunities *run* far away from negative people. Positive emotions create an atmosphere around us for God to speak and for creativity and determination to manifest in our character. This is learning to be led by the inside— becoming strong in spirit and making your own environment, instead of your environment making you!

FILTERING EVERY EMOTION THROUGH HIS FEELINGS

Many, many times the Bible talks about seeking God's face. When we desire to look at other people's faces, we are looking for a number of clues about where their focus is and, more importantly, *what they are feeling*. When the Bible urges us to seek the face of God, it actually means that we should be constantly seeking God's emotions. We must be open to them and easily yielded to their direction. Remember, God's emotions are always based on truth and are catalysts for His actions. They are never out of control, but only give life and expression to the truth.

So how do we activate this concept of seeking the face of God, the emotions of God? First, we do it by checking inside constantly. Like the question, "What would Jesus do?" we ask, "What does the Spirit of God feel? How does He view this situation?" This can really make a difference. We may be very emotionally charged about certain situations, but if we will stop for a moment, we will see that He feels very differently about them.

I remember one time I was very upset about a situation and had an argument with my wife (before we were married). I was so frustrated because I didn't think the situation would ever change, and I wondered if the marriage would ever work because of it. The facts were real, and I cried out to God asking what I could do about it.

Do you know what He did? *He laughed at me.* Seriously, I could feel Him laughing at me from the inside! I stopped in my tracks and got quite upset. I thought I could expect some comfort from the God of all comfort, and I got laughter instead. But before I could ask Him what the meaning of all that was, He stopped and told me things from His perspective. He said, *"There will come a time when you won't even recognize this situation. It will change so much so that to even think back and remember it will simply seem like a dream."* He spoke it with such authority that I knew it was true.

His emotion was based on the truth as He saw it, even when I couldn't see past the emotional fog of the present. I took hold of this "joy set before me" (see Heb. 12:2), and it brought strength to make the right decisions for the future He had planned for me. And do you know what? He was right. I can't even remember what I was so upset about anymore! Thank God I didn't act on what I felt, but on what *He* felt.

The second way to activate this concept is to filter every unexpected emotion that comes at us. *This is an amazing and useful technique.* When an emotion comes upon us suddenly, we must ask God, *"Why* is this happening? Is it from the Spirit of God, or is it from the devil? Or is it from the spiritual atmosphere of where I am at?" Asking the right questions about what we are sensing gives us the alertness to react correctly. "Is it something to resist? Or is it something to actively participate with to effectively do the will of God?"

We were originally created to respond emotionally to spiritual stimulus. Our minds still have that capacity. This is why demonic manifestations often involve emotions! Our emotions still connect with the spiritual realm, and if we will simply stop and analyze the source of these feelings instead of simply reacting irrationally, we can become very sharp in the spirit. *Why* do we feel lonely, frustrated, joyful, energized, nervous, fearful, lustful, sad, compassionate, angry, and so forth? Once we can develop this capacity to always check on the inside at the first emotional sense—seeking His face continually—we become people who can never be emotionally manipulated by other people or by situations again. When this response becomes second nature to us, we become true forces to be reckoned with in the realm of the spirit.

So to continue our training, we must first perfect the "I *will*" emotion exercises. When we can fire them in the right direction at will, then we can follow up in the situations of life. We ask what the Spirit of God feels and how to filter and respond to the emotional forces that are coming at us on a daily basis. It is time for us to get out of the soap opera dramatics of being emotionally controlled; instead we need to use our emotions as fuel for good works to the glory of God.

"EMOTIONS" REVIEW

1. Emotions are identified as the "biggest" part of our souls because they are the most _____ part and have an ability to _____ the rest of the elements of our souls in a spectacular way.

2. _____ has emotions—feelings like joy, sorrow, peace, anger, urgency, jealousy, and compassion. The Bible is full of stories of how people used emotions—for God's glory! *Describe some of the ways Jesus released His emotions.*

3. _____ emotions will _____ us! They force us to live by their dictates, and they possess our mouths and wills.

4. The _____ _____ behind most people's lives is an addiction to emotional feelings.

5. We can spend years repairing the damage ungodly emotions do in just a few moments through our _____.

6. The first key to controlling our emotions is to _____ them. God constantly told people: "Do not _____."

7. Emotions, without the Word of God to give them substance, become _____ decision-makers!

8. When we _____ our _____, we change our _____.

9. Read Psalm 42:5. David _____ his emotions to hope in God.

10. In Philippians 4:4, Paul shows that he had learned the _____ of proper emotional control.

11. Emotions, like military weapons, must be fired in the _____ _____!

12. (a) We grab hold of our emotions by boldly _____ words like, "I _____!"

    (b) Think of five varied emotions, and boldly vocalize them with a scriptural action or attitude similar to what is described on pages 62-63. You will have a chance to write down these thoughts and others at the end of this review.

13. Until our emotions are properly trained, *what we feel is not*_____! The _____ of God is _____.

14. We must push our emotions into _____ through our forceful confession out loud. If we push our emotions to feel the right way, they will eventually change!

15. Emotions are primarily to give _____ and _____ to our faith in God's character and Word.

16. (a) Positive emotions _____ an atmosphere around us for _____ to speak.

    (b) Write down sentences about what you want your emotions to do. Be creative and use statements that actually stir up and direct your emotions in a godly way. Think of situations that may have provoked you in a negative emotional pattern in the past and use the Scripture to find a proper emotion to motivate the proper action.

    _____

    _____

_____

_____

_____

_____

_____

_____

_____

_____

_____

_____

_____

_____

_____

_____

(c) Expressively *declare* your sentence with that emotion! It may seem like acting, but that is because you are in charge, not your emotions! What you feel is not _____; what the Word of God says is _____!

CHAPTER 5

INTELLECT/REASONING

God is an intelligent God. He gave humankind the same kind of intelligence for wonderful purposes. He designed our intellect to first of all have the joy of discovering His creation. There is a certain thrill in seeing the orderly hand of God in creation and His laws. This sense of discovery was to lead to a greater experience of executing His Word and implementing His Word practically!

THE HIDDEN CODE—GOD'S
WAY OF THINKING

There is so much He does not have to tell us because creation itself tells us the way He thinks (see Ps. 19:1-4). For this reason, Jesus used parables from nature and its laws to demonstrate the way the Kingdom of God operates. This tells us time and time again that God is a systematic, intelligent God of knowledge, understanding, counsel, and wisdom. For example, when God tells us to go to a particular nation, He expects us to use our brains based on the information that He has already brought into our paths to get passports or to ask the proper questions to know what we need to know about going there! God *expects* our intellect to be used and to grow.

THE PRIDE OF A CORRUPT MIND

However, an ungodly intellect will rebel against God. It will constantly challenge Him, will think it knows better, or will simply refuse to obey any command of God until it understands everything to its satisfaction. This is a clear case of pride. It will create pride in its track record of good decisions or knowledge gained. "If I don't know something about it already, it probably isn't important." The ungodly intellect will do its best to reason its way out of obedience and will refuse to submit to the simple commands of God. People who think this way tend to stand out because they are usually quite argumentative concerning anything about God. They don't want to *learn* anything about God because it might cause them to have to admit they are wrong about the most foundational issues of life. That is usually too painful for an ungodly intellect to face.

PRIDE IN THE PEW AND PULPIT

But it is not only non-church-going people who can have an ungodly intellect! There are religious people who have had their intellects crystallized to various degrees of ungodliness. Examples of these are the people whom Jesus confronted the most—the Pharisees. They served God by their intellects, not by their spirits. If anyone brought any knowledge about God that didn't fit into their minds, they immediately rejected it. It didn't even matter if their Scriptures agreed with it. These kinds of people are definitely still around today. Their dispositions are evident, first of all, because of their defensive attitudes toward new knowledge about God or simply toward knowledge they already know, but just don't do. They are usually cynical and don't wait to judge something by the clear counsel of the Word or by the fruits, but immediately judge by appearances. *They ask questions to substantiate their doubts rather than to substantiate stronger faith in God's Word and His character.* They have no new openness for God to confirm His Word and love in a new and fresh way in the world. Most importantly, they have no hunger to obey God in a way that they have never done before.

ACKNOWLEDGE THE SOURCE OF KNOWLEDGE

How do we line up our intellects to flow with God? First of all, we must understand that we do not know everything. He is God; we are not. We must also humble our intellects to acknowledge God's perfect intellect in every situation. Proverbs 3:5-6 is the best antidote for an ungodly intellect. *"Trust in the Lord with all your heart, and lean not on your own understanding; in all your ways acknowledge Him, and He shall direct your paths."*

Here is a great instruction—ask God questions! Many actually never do that, usually for two reasons: first, because they think they know the answer already, and second, because they don't think God will answer. Both reasons are faulty. There is always something about every situation that we may not know. We must ask the right questions and then know that God is not trying to keep all the information to Himself. He wants to share His knowledge with anyone who will believe He will answer our requests for knowledge!

We have to be open for new revelation about *any* topic. Also, there will be times where we will *not* be told everything right away, but as we obey the instructions by faith, we will understand more fully. *What we don't get by revelation, we will get by obedience in the situation.* Jesus Himself said there were some things He wanted to share with His disciples, but that they were not able to handle it just yet. However, He said that when the Holy Spirit came, He would tell them of these things (see John 16:12-13; 1 Cor. 2:9-10). The Holy Spirit knows the right timing for us to know certain sensitive information. We must trust Him!

READY TO OBEY; WILLING TO CHANGE

It is so important to train our minds to be yielded and obedient to God's Word. Jesus said it like this, *"If anyone wills to do His [the Father's] will, he shall know concerning the doctrine, whether it is from God or whether I speak on My own authority"* (John 7:17). Once our minds are made up to do God's will, no matter what it is, revelation and understanding will come to us. As we read the Word of God, we must open up our minds to understand its concepts and situations in a fresh way. Then we make sure we petition God for further revelation and accuracy. We don't know it like we may think we do. We must stay humble. Job thought he knew so much about God and life until he met God face-to-face, and then God began to unload questions and understanding upon Job like a machine gun. In the end, Job could only say:

> *I know You can do everything, and that no purpose of Yours can be withheld from You. You asked, "Who is this who hides counsel without knowledge?" Therefore I have uttered what I did not understand, things too wonderful for me, which I did not know...I have heard of You by the hearing of the ear, but now my eye sees You. Therefore I abhor myself, and repent in dust and ashes* (Job 42:2-3;5-6).

Let our minds be ready to change in the light of seeing God's truth.

HUMILITY TEST

For a practical exercise, get a sheet of paper. Draw a large circle on it. Let everything within that circle represent all the knowledge that can be known, all the knowledge past, present, and future. It contains all the knowledge concerning the sciences—of Earth (including every animal, plant, mineral, element, and biological and chemical law), astronomy, physics (every field of study), computers (every technological discovery and advance), medical (every field), and so forth. It contains all knowledge concerning humans (complete history, every detail of relationships, all the arts, and so forth) and all knowledge concerning the spiritual realm and God, as well as all knowledge concerning every book that has been written, knowledge of every single course that could possibly be taught in every university on Earth, every event that has occurred within the history of Earth, and so forth. All of this is represented within that circle.

Now with that in mind, I want you to mark a line across the circle, defining a section that represents the amount of knowledge you personally possess. Would you draw a line halfway across? Maybe a quarter of the way? If you are honest, you would probably only draw the tiniest dot somewhere in the midst of that circle. Now look at it. God thoroughly sees, remembers, and understands all that is possible within that circle of knowledge *and* everything that will be added to it in the future.

OUR CONTINUAL NEED FOR HELP

This is the same God who says:

> *My son, if you receive my words, and treasure my commands within you, so that you incline your ear to wisdom, and apply your heart to understanding; yes, if you cry out for discernment, and lift up your voice for understanding, if you seek her as silver, and search for her as for hidden treasures; then you will understand the fear of the Lord and find the knowledge of God. For the Lord gives wisdom; from His mouth come knowledge and understanding;* (Proverbs 2:1-6).

The apostle Paul put it into praise by saying:

Oh the depth of the riches both of the wisdom and knowledge of God! How unsearchable are His judgments and His ways past finding out! "For who has known the mind of the Lord? Or who has become His counselor? Or who has first given to Him and it shall be repaid to him?" For of Him and through Him and to Him are all things, to whom be glory forever. Amen (Romans 11:33-36).

Let's put that paper up on the wall, and every time we look at it, let it remind us to believe God continually for greater wisdom, knowledge, and understanding—knowing that there is so much that we don't know and need to know. Let's remind ourselves, "If there is anything good that *I do* know, it is how to ask and believe God for help! If I knew one hundred times more than I do now, but didn't know how to do that, I would be missing the most important knowledge that I could have—knowledge of how to connect with the one who knows everything!" Even if we do not have all the fish in the world, thank God that we have a fishing pole by which we can get the fish we need!

Let's practice declaring out loud with all our hearts, *"Father, help me! Please show me what to do! I need Your knowledge, wisdom, and understanding to be revealed to me! I thank You and believe to receive it now!"*

If we will freely focus and release our requests from our hearts to Him, God will freely reveal the wisdom from His heart to us. Go ahead and do it. Let's break free from fear and pride of how silly it looks, disregard what others might think (if they were smart, they would do it too), and do it without any regard for our so-called image of "self-respectability." This will for sure keep us humble. And to the humble, God will give His grace (supernatural empowerment). So next time our brains get a bit uncomfortable or try to mock new knowledge of God, even from "foolish" sources (see 1 Cor. 1:25-29), we must not lean on our own understanding, but acknowledge God and let Him direct our paths.

"LET US REASON TOGETHER..."

After we are well-practiced in this, our intellects can be a great tool of God. In the Book of Acts, the apostles submitted their minds to God's Word no matter what tradition taught. They reasoned things out *with* the Holy Spirit and came to wise conclusions. *"For it seemed good to the Holy Spirit and to us, to lay upon you no greater burden than these necessary things..."* (Acts 15:28). This is a great skill our intellects can have—it is the joy of discovering the Holy Spirit's thinking processes and the peace of being able to simply agree with Him! But this doesn't come easily; it demands our being diligent with the previously discussed foundation of training our intellects.

SECRETS OF A TRUE CUTTING-EDGE LEADER

As a leader, it is important to have a well-trained intellect. Accepting blindly everything people say will never make us the leaders we need to be. Paul knew this. He told Timothy, *"Consider what I say, and may the Lord give you understanding in all things"* (2 Tim. 2:7). We must listen to the teaching, but seek the Lord so our intellects will know how it can be applied more fully. This even applies to this training; there are a lot of practical things in this book, but only God can address specific aspects of it to each of us personally.

Behind *every* intellectual person is a root motivator. No matter how intellectual and knowledgeable people are, there are core beliefs that guide their search for knowledge and their use of knowledge. The key is not in understanding the *content* of people's thinking, but in understanding their *way* of thinking. Even before most people start reasoning, they usually have a goal in mind. Sadly, the truth is not often the goal; instead, they want to prove themselves right. Once again, is this not pride?

The Bible records that Moses was one of the most humble people (see Num. 12:3). God knew he was the best leader, even though almost everyone he led seemed to think differently. The secret to his leadership was not his speaking ability or great faith or bold confidence—he seemed to lack those qualities from the beginning. But Psalm 103:7 gives the surprising secret to his ability to lead: *"He made known His ways to Moses, His acts to the children of Israel."* Moses simply grew to understand how God thought. He daily spent time in the tabernacle of meeting seeking God, immersing himself in God's thoughts and words. The Israelites saw the mighty acts, but Moses knew the *source* of them. The source was God's motivations, His *ways* of thinking!

Moses even used this information "against" God when Moses interceded for Israel! He reminded God of the way He thought (His ways) and how God should act because of this (see Num. 14:11-19). This does not come overnight, but Moses took the time and discipline to mold his intellect to mimic God's ways. This is why God would back up Moses' leadership whenever it was challenged. Moses' goal was not that Moses was proved right; his root motivator was to show that the Lord was right. I think God chose his poor speaking ability, his poor self-image, his poor organizational skills because Moses would never have the justification to say, "I just knew I was great after all!" All he would be able to point to was simply letting God be right. He really wanted God to be magnified above all.

INTELLIGENCE FREED FROM SELFISHNESS

With this as our core motivator, we can reason with the Holy Spirit, and our reasoning will be clean from selfish motivation. Remember the first sign of devilish wisdom?

But if you have bitter envy and self-seeking in your hearts, do not boast and lie against the truth. This wisdom does not descend from above, but is earthly, sensual, demonic. For where envy and self-seeking exist, confusion and every evil thing are there (James 3:14-16).

But what is the sign of a godly intellect?

But the wisdom that is from above is first pure, then peaceable, gentle, willing to yield, full of mercy and good fruits, without partiality and without hypocrisy (James 3:17).

I didn't understand this for a while because it sounds like true wisdom means that we allow ourselves to be run over by other people! Does it mean we just yield to anyone or have peace with anyone? But we must recognize it is first *pure*—that means it is not primarily focused horizontally toward pleasing humans, but true wisdom is focused on God's interests *first*. It seeks peace on God's terms, not people's. It yields easily to God's Word and Spirit. Then it shows goodness and mercy to people. And it stays *consistent*. This is because God's ways do not change!

This is the wisdom that Moses had, and we can discover the method he used—saturating himself in God's presence daily and memorizing God's Word. (He wrote the first five books of the Bible without a tape recorder, computer, or notepad and pen. That is a lot of memorizing!) He saw the greatness of God and just wanted Him to be number one. That was the pathway for his intellect to think along God's ways of thinking.

"INTELLECT/REASONING" REVIEW

1. God is systematic, intelligent, has all knowledge, understanding, counsel, and wisdom. He _____ our intellect to be used and to grow.

2. The _____ intellect reasons its way out of obedience and refuses to submit to the commands of God.

3. The religious people (Pharisees) serve God by their intellects, not by their _____. Their attitude is to judge by appearances, and they don't *do* the Word.

4. (a) Some people ask questions to substantiate their _____ rather than to have stronger _____ in God.

   (b) Identify the differences between a critical person asking a question and a child asking a question.

5. Read Proverbs 3:5-6. It tells us to _____ God questions. He wants to share His knowledge with us.

6. Two reasons people do *not* ask God questions are:

   1) _____

   _____

   _____

   2) _____

   _____

   _____

7. We have to be _____ for revelation about any topic. There will be times when we will not be told everything right away, but as we obey by _____, we will understand more fully.

8. What we don't get by _____, we will get by obedience in the situation.

9. Read John 7:17. As you read the Word, be open to understand its concepts and situations in a _____way. Then _____ God for further revelation and accuracy!

10. Read Job 42:2-3, 5-6. If you have not done so already, complete the humility test now. What does your completed test reveal?

11. Let our minds be ready to change in the light of _____ God's truth. Read Romans 11:33-36.

12. To the _____ God will give His _____ (supernatural empowerment).

13. The apostles submitted their minds to God's Word, not tradition. They then were able to _____ things out _____ the Holy Spirit (see Acts 15:28).

14. _____ to teaching but _____ the Lord so our intellects can learn how to apply it (see 2 Tim. 2:7).

15. There is a root motivator behind every intellect. The key is not in understanding the _____ of people's thinking, but in understanding their _____ of thinking.

16. (a) Moses grew to understand how God _____ (see Ps. 103:7). The Israelites saw God's mighty acts, but Moses knew the _____ of them.

(b) How did this happen for Moses? How can this happen for us as well?

17. The _____ of a godly intellect is shown in James 3:17. Godly wisdom is not _____ focused on pleasing humans, but focused on God's interests _____.

18. The _____ for us to think along God's way of thinking is to want Him to be number one!

CHAPTER 6

MEMORY

O ur memories hold the powerful key of self-identity. If we had some kind of accident in which we lost our memories, we would be lost in this world—even if we never left our homes. Our memory is our most powerful tool of identity and the base for all our decision-making abilities. Everything we are, every experience we have had, every book we have read, every conversation we have had, every lecture we have attended, every sensation and emotion we have experienced— is filed away in our unique, complex memories. We think we are who we are because of this accumulation and configuration of our memories. We decide what we decide based on our memories of past decisions (of ourselves and others) and facts stored there. This is the part of our souls that can be the most difficult to sort out. However, *it will be the most vital to sort out* because every other part of our souls will draw on the resources of the memory to be able to function!

AMMUNITION STOREHOUSE OF THE SOUL

God created humankind with a marvelous capacity to use our memories. Science tells us that we only use a small portion of the capacity that our physical brains possess. Even if we did have a serious accident that caused us to lose our memory of how to do some important conscious motor skills, it is still possible to relearn them because of this latent mental capacity. The Holy Spirit has a special working relationship with this part of our souls based on this promise:

> *But the Helper, the Holy Spirit, whom the Father will send in My Name, He will teach you all things, and bring to your remembrance all things that I said to you* (John 14:26).

Because our memories are the source for the rest of our souls to draw upon for proper functioning, it is so vital for the Holy Spirit to be the one in charge of our mental hard drives. He will be the one to pull up the most vital information that we need for victory in any situation. That is fantastic news. However, there is a catch; there must be a proper uploading of information that the Holy Spirit can use! If we never upload any of the Word of God into our memories, the Holy Spirit has very little to draw upon for use.

TREASURE VAULT OR HOUSE OF HORRORS?

The danger of an ungodly memory is this: all information that is set before our eyes will be uploaded and stored, regardless of whether it is true or not. This new information *will* affect our future behavior patterns. Ungodly memories can also make us prisoners of the past. They will paralyze our progress in the plans that God has for us. If all our memories will pull up is past failures, mistakes, offenses, and so forth, how can our lives ever get any better? Our memories can crystallize ungodly emotions (cynicism, bitterness, depression, lust, fear, and so forth) into our personalities. This is such a dangerous state to be in! There is no way for destiny to be fulfilled because this will surely poison all present and future attempts for success. This is because our memories have now become strongholds against God. They have now become false standards for disobedience and unbelief. "This is the way it happened before, and this is how I learned to survive and be happy with it, so this is how I am. Period." How could it be otherwise? We were never programmed any differently.

VIRUSES INFECT THE HARD DRIVE AND PROGRAMS

Ungodly memories become like a virus factory to the rest of our souls. For example: If a man has had an experience with rejection early in life (like parents or friends mocking, criticizing, or verbally abusing him) and that issue was never treated, it will grow until it becomes a stronghold of fear. Then, if this root of rejection and fear is never effectively dealt with, it will eventually crystallize into a spirit of rebellion. "I'm too shy and afraid to do that" is what he used to say; now it becomes, "I don't *have* to do that because I don't want to." The fear has caused him to now become a slave to it and to rebel against anything that would make him disobey that spirit of fear.

With each year of this not being dealt with, the memory becomes more and more poisoned because this attitude is being reinforced by other people who accept it as part of that man's personality. The next stage is even more scary, however, as this rebellion can evolve into a spirit of hatred and even murder. The man then no longer wants to just rebel against the voices that want him to disobey his spirits of rejection and fear in the circumstances of life; he now want to permanently cut off those voices! This spirit of murder is sometimes manifested in an actual killing, but it will often manifest in other ways such as slander, backbiting, ridicule, condemnation, rejection, and rage.

This entire process can take many years, but once the memory is crystallized, it will take a serious miracle to break down these strongholds. This is why it is so important to deal with negative memories as soon as possible. Even with children, we must work to instill the principles of the Word of God within them; genuine experiences with the Spirit of God in their minds will be powerful enough to keep their minds healthy and poised for an unhindered destiny.

WELLSPRING OF STRENGTH AND LIFE

The potential of the memory is just as powerful for good as it could be for bad. A trained memory will be a catalyst for faith, thanksgiving, joy, hope, love, and courage. God constantly tells His people to *remember* the words He spoke to them. Forty-five times in Deuteronomy alone God commands His people to remember the Word of God. More than that, He tells us that our memories of His works in the past will become our faith for the same things happening in the present and future.

He has made His wonderful works to be remembered... (Psalm 111:4).

And I said, "This is my anguish; **but I will remember** *the years of the right hand of the Most High." I will remember the works of the Lord; surely I will remember Your wonders of old* (Psalm 77:10-11).

My son, give attention to my words....Do not let them depart from your eyes; keep them in the midst of your heart; **for they are life** *to those who find them, and* **health** *to all their flesh* (Proverbs 4:20-22).

Bless the Lord, O my soul, **and forget not** *all His benefits...* (Psalm 103:2).

Whenever the memory of what the Holy Spirit has done in our lives is stirred up, so is the gift of the Holy Spirit! *"Therefore* **I remind you** *to stir up the gift of God which is in you..."* (2 Tim. 1:6). Just as ungodly memories can crystallize us into the twisted shape of bitterness or rejection, we can also train our memories to program our lives into a pattern of thanksgiving, faith, rejoicing, positive speaking, and love. Our memories don't know to do anything else except get into line with what the Holy Spirit has done and has taught us to do! *This attracts God's power very easily.*

POWER TO SHUT ONE DOOR AND OPEN A NEW DOOR

If we are in a process of dealing with ungodly memories from the past that keep coming up and drowning our minds, *we must know that we have authority over our memories.* The apostle Paul wrote in Philippians 3:13-14:

> *Brethren, I do not count myself to have apprehended; but one thing I do, forgetting those things which are behind and reaching forward to those things which are ahead, I press toward the goal for the prize of the upward call of God in Christ Jesus.*

Paul knew the danger—how an ungodly memory could paralyze and hold him back from his destiny; he took authority over his memory and chose instead to remember those things that would keep him reaching forward in life. This is what we must do also. "I choose to forget those things that keep me bound to the past! I choose to reject thought patterns that resulted in wrong behaviors! I choose to focus on what God has spoken about my future! I choose to forget what others have said about me. What does *God* say?"

What is our hope? It is our blueprint for our faith to manifest it in the future. If we have done wrong in the past, we must repent, make amends, humble ourselves, ask for forgiveness, and forgive those who have hurt and offended us. We must set ourselves free!

God promises to do the same; He does not condemn us for our past. He also chooses to forget it! *"I, even I, am He who blots out your transgressions for My own sake; and I will not remember your sins"* (Isa. 43:25). What are God's thoughts for us? *"For I know the thoughts that I think toward you, says the Lord, thoughts...to give you a future and a hope"* (Jer. 29:11).

We must make a decision like the apostle Paul made. The best is yet to come. This is where we must connect our godly memories with a godly imagination in order to align with everything God wants to do for our future. But we will talk more about that important topic later.

THE BACKBONE OF OUR FAITH

It is absolutely vital to have good memories. Our ability to have faith is directly related to our ability to have good memories. God's faithfulness is based on the fact that *He remembers* His Word. *Our faith is shown in **how we remember** (and declare and demonstrate to God that we remember!) the promises and commands that He cannot forget!*

> *Can a woman forget her nursing child, and not have compassion on the son of her womb? Surely they may forget, yet I will not forget you* (Isaiah 49:15).

On the other hand, every time God's people sinned, it was because of a collective weakness in their memories.

> *How often they provoked Him in the wilderness, and grieved Him in the desert! Yes, again and again they tempted God, and limited the Holy One of Israel. They did not remember His power...* (Psalm 78:40-42).

All throughout biblical history, both revivals and failures were always initiated by the quality of the people's memories of God's Word and works. *Always.* Even in modern times, numerous men and women of God who were used greatly have fallen simply because they failed to remember their roots. They didn't remember or no longer valued what they first did to achieve their success in God. *It is a sobering fact that God will give someone an instruction early in life, and without repeating Himself, expect that person to remember and do it 20 to 40 years later.*

> *Remember therefore from where you have fallen; repent and do the first works, or else I will come to you quickly and remove your lampstand from its place—unless you repent* (Revelation 2:5).

This is why I appreciate so much those pioneers of ministry today who remember, preach, and practice what God told them so long ago. It seems that decades of meditation, practice, testing, and development of those principles memorized long ago makes them so much more powerful and sharp today. Without having a quality memory throughout life, there is no way they would have the quality of leadership and respect they have in their latter years. Because of the quality of their memories, *their words carry weight that other people's don't.*

We must require ourselves to have good memories. *We must believe God for a good memory!*

TRAIN IT HARD; TRAIN IT WELL

Many people complain about not having a good memory. When it comes time for God to pull up something that He has taught them, they just can't seem to find it in the midst of the garbage they have already accumulated within their memories. They say they have a bad memory. This is a fact we must know: *There are no bad memories, just untrained memories.*

This exercise will take a longer process, but the rewards are great. First, you must find a small quality notebook. Next, I suggest you find several different colors of pens. What you must do is this: Find out different scriptural topics that you know you are not strong in. For example: How many Scriptures can you remember on faith—*right now.*

If you come up with a blank after 30 seconds or just a weak, mumbled phrase from some portion of the Bible, you need to find some good, strong inspiring Scriptures on faith. Put "Faith" as a title for a few pages of your notebook in a certain color, and then go search your Bible until you find some good verses to fill up those pages.

Please don't cheat by cutting and pasting from some computer program or photocopying someone else's topical Scripture book. The effectiveness of this exercise will be lost. (See Deuteronomy 17:18-20.) Also, please write as neatly as possible. Do the same for other topics such as love, salvation, victory, healing, protection, wisdom, prosperity, holiness, freedom from fear, God's blessing, forgiveness, righteousness, the Holy Spirit, and so forth—whatever you think you need to be stronger in.

FRIENDS AND ENEMIES—GLAD TO HELP YOU

Also, it will help to have some other people tell you what your problems are. (I know that takes courage, but sometimes you just can't see it without someone else telling you.) Why should you do that? It is because of your thinking patterns that you do what you do and you are the way you are. *"For as a man thinks in his heart, so is he"* (Prov. 23:7a). Thank God for your errors because they reveal a faulty memory and thinking pattern. So when other people tell you your faults (by the way, please get someone who can tell you the truth), that's it. You can now look for the Scriptures to solve that problem, and you will never be the same again. *"How can a young man cleanse his way? By taking heed according to Your Word"* (Ps. 119:9).

FLEXING MEMORY MUSCLES; MAKING A PATHWAY

Now what do you do after that? You take that notebook and begin to meditate on it. Take it with you everywhere. Challenge yourself:

"Memory, recall a Scripture on success (or some other topic)—now!" Pull it up from within you and begin to quote it. If you can't remember it, look it up in your notebook. Then quote it again, this time without looking. What is happening is that within your brain you are building a new neural pattern highway. You are also closing down negative neural thought-pattern roads through disuse, as well as connecting them with positive "off-ramps" when needed. When you are constantly remembering Scriptures on faith, healing, wisdom, and so forth, you make it easier and easier to think that way *for the rest of your life*. It will also help you to find some friends who are willing to become "training partners" (just like at a gym) who will push and challenge you to sharpen each other's "swords of the Spirit" on various topics. It is amazing how this back-and-forth "game" can give your spirit a surprising boost! Try it!

TRAIN FOR LIFE; READY IN AN INSTANT

We must not stop doing this after a few weeks. We need to make this memory workout a continual program for life in order to keep our memories healthy and strong. The reason for this is that we are constantly having information pushed at us every day. Our memories are going to take some things in whether we like it or not; we cannot let godly food for our memories become deficient at any time in our lives or else we will have only fresh, negative food to serve the rest of our souls. We must constantly challenge our memories on various topics and answer them with Scriptures that we have memorized. We never know when it will come in handy or when the Holy Spirit will need to use that "sword" quickly.

When Jesus was tempted by the devil to turn stones into bread (see Luke 4), He began right away to pull up all the Scripture files He had in His memory on bread: *Bread...bread...hmmm....OK—got it!* "It is written, 'Man shall not live by **bread** alone, but by every word of God'" (Luke 4:4).

Then the devil tried to get Jesus to worship him, so Jesus pulled up all the memory files on worship: *Worship...worship...OK, this is a good one:* "*Get behind Me, Satan! For it is written, 'You shall* **worship** *the Lord your God, and Him only you shall serve'*" (Luke 4:8).

This is how Jesus trained His memory to work so that at the time when He was under pressure, He could pull up a Scripture on any topic He needed to. We must not let our memories be our weakest link, but our greatest asset and the Holy Spirit's tool for our success.

EXPANDING OUR ABILITIES

However, we shouldn't limit our memories to Scripture only. We must exercise our memories' capacity to remember many things throughout the day—names, places, events, facts. We can't let our memories be lazy by just brushing it off if we forget people's names or some important facts. Instead, we must be attentive, speaking to our memories and demanding them to remember and recall clearly! God wants us to live an accurate life. The Holy Spirit will lead us into *all* truth (see John 16:13), and that includes every aspect of life. The capacity of the human mind (especially empowered by the Holy Spirit) is immense; through disciplined training, we can remember far more than we ever thought we could. God has not unveiled our potential yet.

The last thing I want to say about this topic of memory is that our memories do not have to dictate who we are. We are not our personalities, our experiences, or our collections of acquired knowledge. Take hope with this thought—*no one knows who we are yet, not even us.* Only our Creator God knows who we are, and who we are will only come alive through this process of developing our spirit life. In the presence of God and in communion with the Holy Spirit, the seeds of destiny He has planted within our spirits will begin to sprout, and we will become more than we ever thought possible.

"MEMORY" REVIEW

1. (a) The part of our souls that can be the most difficult to sort out is the _____. It is the most _____ however, because every other part of our souls draws upon it to function! That's why the Holy Spirit needs to be in charge of our "hard drives."

   (b) How does John 14:26 relate to your memory?

2. Our memories can become _____ against God and false standards for disobedience and unbelief.

3. A root of rejection and fear can become a spirit of _____, or eventually even a spirit of _____ or _____! It is important to deal with _____ memories as soon as possible.

4. A _____ memory can be a catalyst for _____. God tells us to _____ His works and words (see Ps. 77:10-11; 103:2; 111:4; Prov. 4:20-22; Ps. 103:2).

5. We can train our memories to program our lives into a pattern of thanksgiving, faith, rejoicing, positive speaking, and love. This _____ God's power very easily.

6. (a) We have _____ over our memories (see Phil. 3:13-14). Reach forward in life by saying "I _____ what is behind. I _____ toward the mark of the _____ call!"

   (b) What does God promise in Isaiah 43:25?

7. Our faith is _____ in _____ _____ _____ God's Word (and declare and _____ to God that we _____) His promises and commands (see Isa. 49:15; Ps. 78:41-42a; Rev. 2:5).

8. _____ of ourselves to have a good memory. _____ God for a good memory!

9. (a) There are no bad memories, just _____ memories.

   (b) Explain some of the ways that can help you train your memory.

10. It is because of our _____ patterns that we do what we do and we are the way we are (see Prov. 23:7a). In a journal or notebook, write out three weaknesses you have had issues with. Then look for and write down Scriptures that directly address these issues. Memorize them!

11. We must _____ on Scriptures throughout the day so that we will build new neural pattern highways in our _____ and close down negative neural thought-pattern roads through disuse, as well as connect them with positive "off-ramps."

12. Make this _____ _____ a continual program for life to keep your memory healthy and strong. *How did Jesus train His memory?* (See Luke 4.) Let your memory be your greatest asset and the Holy Spirit's tool for your success!

13. _____ your memory throughout the day. Be _____. Speak to your memory and demand that it remember and recall clearly. Don't say, "I can't remember"; say "I _____ _____!" *How can the Holy Spirit help you in this?* (See John 16:13.)

14. (a) Make sure that you have found a good journal or notebook to write down Scriptures where you need to "bulk up" your memory and life. Find at least three good Scriptures for each topic.

    (b) What topics do you have in mind so far?

(A good way to increase your Scripture list and depth is through doing your daily Bible reading plan with your notebook next to you. When you find a Scripture that relates to your topic, you can immediately put it into your notebook. This also helps create a full context for that Scripture.)

CHAPTER 7

IMAGINATION

The imagination is an incredibly powerful component to spirit life and one of my favorites to train. I can't express that strongly enough.

MENTAL TELEPORTATION

The human imagination is the preparation tool for building into the realm of the spirit. It is the gift of God to people to take us places before we get there, to do things before we actually experience them, and to have things before we physically possess them. This is not fantasy; it is preparation. Every invention of humankind began as a possibility in someone's imagination. Every architectural wonder that has been built once existed only in the imagination. Every Olympic gold-medal winner's imagination was set on winning. Every successful achievement or product required the positive imagination of the achiever. It may be true that many people imagined the same achievements, but the success of these achievements always belonged to the people whose imaginations gripped them the strongest.

When we develop our imaginations, we develop our future. That is a fact. However, even though this is true, it's sad that very few schools will have a class for training the imagination!

NO LIMITS

God Himself created the imagination so that *whatever the mind conceives, it can achieve.* Even in Genesis there is a surprising illustration of this truth. In chapter 11 it tells of a people who gathered together to make a plan to build a tower to reach into Heaven. They imagined a people who would be unified under a central form of worship (but not to God), language, economy, and culture. God Himself came down and saw what they were doing and saw their mindset regarding their project and declared:

> *Indeed the people are one and they all have one language, and this what they begin to do; now nothing that they propose to do will be withheld from them* (Genesis 11:6).

This was directly against God's instruction for humankind to spread across the Earth. God changed the languages of the people so they would be forced to separate and develop communities all over the Earth. The point is this: The Bible admits that these people even had the power to achieve something against God's will because their imaginations were set and unified to accomplish it. If God Himself hadn't stopped it, it would have happened.

The imagination is powerful. The development of the imagination does two things for us. First, it increases the borders of our minds. "I have never done it before" becomes "I *could* do it this way!" Second, it breaks mental limitations. "I can't do it" becomes "I know I *can* do it!" The question is: are our imaginations set on something godly or ungodly?

WHAT WE "SEE" IS WHAT WE GET

A negative imagination can be used to create negative mental pictures of who we think we are. This is what is meant by "having a negative self-image." It comes from the imagination being programmed the wrong way. "I'm too fat...too skinny...too poor...not smart...and so forth." This has even birthed a profession of psychologists who try to get into people's imaginations to try to unravel the negative mindsets they have. The reason these psychologists get paid so much is because of how important the imagination is to a person's quality of life! If the imagination is not fixed, the person could be doomed to disaster.

The Bible calls these negative imaginations "strongholds" (see 2 Cor. 10:4-5). These strongholds, in effect, *control people's lives.* Here's how: Disobedient and negative actions are driven by the outcomes people imagine (through these strongholds) that their obedience will produce!

For example, it becomes difficult for someone to love others because of imaginations about a particular individual on the receiving end of that love: "If I love that person, they will someday hurt me. They won't love me back. They don't care about me."

In such cases, people only foresee negative scenarios about how others will treat them. *And* because they already have their imaginations set that this is how it is going to be, they are mentally prepared to keep their guard up, keep others at a distance, and act in hostile ways toward their "enemies." *So whatever their minds have conceived, that is what they achieve.* What they protect against is exactly what happens. Because they act in hostile ways, other people likewise react with hostility—and they wonder why their lives are full of strife! The more the strongholds in the imagination are backed up by memories of negative events, the harder life becomes.

BIRTHING BONDAGE...

If we want to change our future, we must develop our imaginations. This is not psychology, mind-over-matter, positive thinking stuff. It is simply understanding the way God created us. A demonic stronghold in our imaginations will destroy our future. The pornography industry generates billions of dollars every year because of the power of people's imaginations to become addicted to pornography. Horror films are totally built around feeding people's fearful imaginations, while romantic films are designed to stimulate the imaginations of people who are inwardly lonely or insecure, causing them to hope for better relationships in the future. Similar things could be said for the rest of the film industry. Negative imaginations have spawned racism, demonic cults, and horrible acts of hatred.

None of these things just "happened" one day. They were developed day by day through strongholds in the imagination. Prisons are filled with people who do not merely have bad memories of the past, but are also imprisoned in their imaginations concerning the future. The high percentage of repeat offenders testifies that this is true! A mistake may be temporary, but a life of future failure comes from a poisoned imagination.

People have gotten sick and have even died because of a negative imagination. People call these kinds of sicknesses "psychosomatic" sicknesses, which means the sickness is not real, but is only in the mind. However, the fact remains that, through the power of a negative imagination, people can take a negative report about a spreading disease and develop such a strong image of that disease in their minds that their bodies manifest the physical symptoms!

...OR BREAKTHROUGH?

Satan has tapped into the power of the imagination to destroy people's lives in so many ways, but know this: *the power of the imagination does not belong to him.* It belongs to those who want to connect its potential with the power of spirit life! When we connect our imagination with the Spirit of God, so many marvelous things can happen. *What happens in our minds will happen in time.* The key is to base it upon the highest potential of a promise or command fulfilled from the Word of God. We can imagine people's souls getting saved. We can imagine family members who are far from God becoming surrounded by God's presence, love, and conviction. We can see them bowing their heads and opening their hearts and mouths to God and see the tears in their eyes. Now see the resolve in their hearts and lives as they lift their heads and eyes to dedicate themselves without shame to serve Jesus. It becomes so easy for them to change...*if we already imagined them becoming that way.*

We can also imagine who *we* are in God's eyes: loved, accepted, His children, forgiven, holy, strong, blessed, provided for, and so much more! How would our lives *and faith* change if our imaginations could grab these things so strongly? We would truly become new creatures (see 2 Cor. 5:17). The problem people have is that they read that the Bible says this and that about them, but their imaginations don't take hold of it! We must stop reading so fast—*stop* and *imagine!* If we read 20 chapters and listen to three teaching CDs, but our *imaginations* don't take hold of it, how can our future behavior look any different? *Imagination and faith work very closely together. Read that again!* (We will explore this more later.)

PREPARE YE THE WAY OF THE LORD

You can imagine yourself laying hands on sick people and seeing them recover! Imagine the healing of lung cancers, high fevers, migraine headaches, knee injuries, and so forth. Be vivid in your imagination! Imagine yourself succeeding in sales, having a better character of diligence, loving bitter people, being blessed financially, improving your family relationships, and having vigorous health!

Imagine your relationship with God improving so that it becomes easy to hear His voice, remember His Word, and praise and love Him throughout the day. Imagine His glory filling your church sanctuary and the hallways of your home. Imagine His presence surrounding you the very moment your mind turns to Him. The moment you open your mouth to pray to Him, imagine that He runs into the room to meet with you!

Why can't you imagine Him that way? With God, as you change your mental picture *of* Him, He can change the experience you have *with* Him. Your imagination doesn't actually change who He is, but the more vivid your imagination becomes regarding the kind of God the Bible says He is, the more your spirit is released to welcome and experience Him that way! If you don't believe me, try it.

SPIRITUAL POWER SWITCHES

Jesus Himself used many illustrations and parables in His teaching. He used them to create mental pictures in the imagination concerning spiritual realities. He knew as soon as people could start using their imaginations according to what they knew of the natural world, directly relating it to spiritual truths, it would empower them to obey God better and also correctly position them for God's blessing.

Therefore I speak to them in parables, because seeing they do not see, and hearing they do not hear, nor do they understand. And in them is the prophecy of Isaiah is fulfilled, which says: "Hearing you will hear and shall not understand, and seeing you will see and not perceive; for the hearts of this people have grown dull. Their ears are hard of hearing, and their eyes they have closed, lest they should see with their eyes and hear with their ears, lest they should understand with their heart and turn, so that I should heal them" (Matthew 13:13-15).

Jesus needed them to use their imaginations in a fresh way so they could start obeying in ways they previously had strongholds in. One time God spoke something very shocking to me. *He told me that even the ordinances such as baptism and communion were actually quite useless without the active engagement of the imagination during these acts.* The Bible gives so many symbols throughout its pages, and those symbols are power switches in the realm of the Spirit when activated by sensitive obedience to the Holy Spirit and the full participation of the imagination.

BUILDING A MENTAL LIGHTNING ROD

The imagination can bring things to life. It is a powerful key to accessing the power of God to heal, bless, and deliver. Every effective healing evangelist has discovered this key. They always dramatically tell a story of healing from the Bible. For example, they may talk about blind Bartimaeus sitting for so many years by the road begging for a few coins to live on (see Luke 18:35-43). The evangelist will make us feel as if we are in Bartimaeus's place, hearing that a good, healing Jesus is about to pass by. He will cause our imaginations to be gripped with the same urgency that gripped Bartimaeus's heart and to have that same determination that *nothing* is going to stop us from getting healed by Jesus *today!* When the whole crowd's imagination has transported them 2000 years back in time to vividly witness and experience an event such as that, miracles always happen. The reason is, as the evangelist would remind them, *"Jesus Christ is the same yesterday, today, and forever"* (Heb. 13:8).

The Spirit of God moves so powerfully during this time because of the promise of Acts 1:8: *"But you shall receive power when the Holy Spirit has come upon you; and you shall be witnesses to Me...."* A witness is someone who has *seen* something. How can people today be actual witnesses of something that has happened 2000 years ago? *Through the power of imagination.* When people's imaginations can vividly picture Jesus doing and saying something that is stated in the Word of God, the Holy Spirit is released to confirm with power that true event that is being imagined!

Faith is based on the eternal truths of the Word of God. Faith works with the imagination because the imagination is what stimulates *hope*. *"Now faith is the substance of **things hoped for**, the evidence of things not seen"* (Heb. 11:1). Once the desired Word-based images in our imaginations reach such a saturation point in our minds, hope explodes upward and shoots out to grab our miracles by faith. Suddenly, what we imagined, we now have! Our pain is gone; our tumors are gone, and so forth. And the funny thing is, it is not really a surprise to us. This is because our imagination of that miracle so saturated our minds that it became easy to believe and receive it.

I COULD SEE THAT COMING

This is why every miracle that Jesus performed didn't surprise Him. His imagination had already seen it happen. In Mark 11, it tells a story of how Jesus cursed a fig tree. Later, when the disciples passed by it, they found it was dried up from the roots. This shocked them, but Jesus was not surprised at all. He simply said:

Have faith in God. For assuredly I say to you, whoever says to this mountain, "Be removed and be cast into the sea," and does

*not doubt in his heart, but believes that those things he says will
be done, he will have whatever he says"* (Mark 11:22-23).

They were shocked at the tree, but Jesus told them to imagine a
mountain being thrown into the sea! He told them that if they would
imagine this strongly in their hearts that it would happen just like
they would say it, *when* they would say it, *it would happen!* What was
He doing when He said this? He was stretching their imaginations
to the furthest limits so their minds could make room for faith. "If I
can imagine something as incredible as my faith moving a mountain,
I can imagine my faith doing so many other things!" As we stretch
the limits on the possibilities of our imaginations, we expand the possibilities of our faith.

WHY CAN'T THAT HAPPEN?

There are so many things that, once the imagination can grab hold
of them, God's Word says our faith can have. In the Dark Ages, very few
people could imagine being saved by faith in Jesus alone. They could
only imagine salvation was through taking sacraments, worshiping so
many saints, saying so many prayers, buying indulgences, and so forth.
But now it is common for anyone to know that simply confessing our
faith in the Lord Jesus Christ for forgiveness and salvation will take us
to Heaven. The Bible also declares that healing and the baptism of the
Holy Spirit are for everyone. Now it is becoming more common for
many to believe these things, but just 100 years ago these things were
scoffed at by most sincere Bible-believing church members and pastors!
*I believe that someday in the near future, raising people from the dead will
be as common as healing a headache.* I know we can all come up with
rules and reasons why that shouldn't be possible, but all that is really

needed is for the imagination to vividly line up with the Word of God (see Matt. 10:7-8; John 11:40; 14:12).

IMAGINATION: FLIGHT SIMULATOR FOR THE WORD

One practical exercise is to begin to imagine a demonstration of a promise of the Word of God in your life. For example, it may be that you know the Word of God promises deliverance from demonic powers. If you have never dealt with this before, using your imagination will be vital for future victory! Sometimes you can even listen to another person's victorious experience of ministering deliverance and through your imagination you can place yourself in their shoes, as if you were the one who was ministering. Imagine the person's face begin to change as the demon manifests to challenge you. Imagine the emotions of fear, hate, jealousy, lust, or pride start coming through the eyes of this person. How would *you* feel at that point? Would you become afraid? Or would you reach down deep inside for the boldness and confidence of the Spirit of God?

You know what you have to do. You choose not to back down in fear. You choose to boldly rebuke that spirit, giving your voice strength and boldness. You command it to come out of that person in the name of Jesus Christ. How does that person react? Maybe that spirit starts to twist in torment inside the person, not wanting to leave, but knowing it must go. Maybe it starts to whine, trying to get you to change your mind. What will you do? Your command becomes even stronger. This person must be set *free!* The holy anger of God rises up inside you and you have no fear as you continue to press in and demand for it to come out *now* until finally the person is released and relieved. He thanks you, and even though he is tired, he is happy and free.

If you have never imagined role-play situations in your mind beforehand, you will freeze in fear or confusion when some surprising situations actually occur—and that's it. You're finished. Your faith, confidence, and spirit just flew out the window! This is why aerospace flight schools will invest in and use flight simulation programs long before someone takes the controls of a multi-million dollar plane. They know that some situations are too costly to try to learn by trial and error. Before you attempt something with God, let your imagination be your flight simulator. My pastor used to say that as he would pray for each meeting, God would show him what would happen beforehand. So when he would get to the meeting, he would simply reenact what he had already seen before in prayer! This ability only comes when the imagination is yielded and ready to be used vividly by the Spirit of God.

GOD EXPECTS US TO EXPECT SUCCESS

Sometimes (or even *many* times) in prayer God can give a picture of something He knows we can do. It could be in school, witnessing to a friend or neighbor, praying for someone who is desperately sick, business, and so forth. Our responsibility is to start to pray in the Spirit and begin to let our imaginations construct that situation into a scenario where we successfully accomplish what God wants us to do.

We must use our imaginations vividly, however! Obedience can be challenging if we have not already thoroughly played out every possibility concerning it in our minds. We must make sure we only use our imaginations for success, *never* failure. Our imaginations must give us every provision for victory. In Numbers 13, Moses sent 12 spies to investigate the Promised Land. Ten came back with a fearful report, saying that they looked like grasshoppers compared to the giants in the land. (Now that was a group of people with winning imaginations.)

Two others, Joshua and Caleb, saw the same thing naturally, but saw something very different in their imaginations! They saw the enemies as bread before them, and the Israelites were going to just eat them up!

Those were the only two who got to possess the Promised Land *even though it was promised to everyone!* (Remember, life in the spirit is our "promised land.") When God gives us promises, He expects us to use our imaginations to see their successful fulfillment—long before we physically do. God said that Joshua and Caleb had *"a different spirit"* (see Num. 14:24). This shows that the imagination-spirit connection is very strong and that the imagination has a powerful impact upon our spiritual abilities and our potential to release them.

AS GOOD AS DONE

Think about this surprising and powerful truth in Matthew 5:28: Jesus said that merely the *imagination of adultery* is just as serious as the physical act! Now that's an example of the power of the imagination in the negative sense. Have you ever thought about it in the positive sense? The mere imagination of healing cancer is just as serious as the physical act! The imagination of raising children that love and serve God is just as serious as the physical act. *Just as a guy could fantasize adultery with any woman, we must be able to imagine with the same passion miracles happening daily in our midst. God would never give more authority and ability to a negative imagination than He would to a positive one!*

OUR TIME MACHINE

Through the imagination we can take Scripture promises into our past, our present, and our future. If we are struggling with memories of failure in our past, we can take Scriptures and strategies into our past mistakes. We can replay the situation in our minds and fix it the way we wish it could have been done. This way we won't repeat the same problem again! We can do the same with what we are struggling with now. Imagine the issues in our present lives being resolved and recreated through God's promises. Now, let's plant our futures with God's promises and plans. With the power of our imaginations, we can actually take control of our past, present, and future!

BEFORE WE TRY IT, *STOP* AND *WIN IT*

The imagination developed and set on the promises of God changes anyone into a champion. The key is to take the time to just *sit* and *imagine*. We should not just *do* things before our imaginations have the chance to travel into those situations first and win the victory beforehand! There is a movie called *Searching for Bobby Fischer* in which a young, talented boy named Josh learns to play chess. His father discovers that he has an incredible ability to play and win so he takes him to a Grandmaster chess tutor to develop him into a champion.

The teacher teaches this boy to think many moves ahead. When there was a sure way to win, he would ask Josh, "Do you see it yet?" Josh could never see it, and it was frustrating him until the teacher swept all the chess pieces off the playing board onto the floor and commanded him to use his imagination—"Now *look!*" He had to train his imagination to see things in a whole new way. Finally, Josh learned to see the victory right after the first few moves of his opponent. In his championship match, Josh even offered a draw to his opponent out of kindness because Josh knew he had already won from the very beginning moves.

This is the confidence we can build in our spiritual lives through the development of our imaginations. We can go into any situation and take it captive for the Lord because we have already seen the victory in the Spirit, because we have developed the capacity of our imagination to receive it. This is why Paul could say, *"Thanks be to God, **who always leads us in triumph** in Christ..."* (2 Cor. 2:14) and *"Yet **in all these things we are more than conquerors** through Him who loved us"* (Rom. 8:37).

Your victories may be a surprise to everybody else, *but never let them be a surprise to you.*

SPEAKING THE HOLY SPIRIT'S LANGUAGE

There is a fine line between the imagination and a gift of the Holy Spirit. In Acts 2:17, Peter tells us that the outpouring of the Spirit is the fulfillment of Joel's prophecy that *"...your young men shall see visions, your old men shall dream dreams."* The Holy Spirit can really use a healthy imagination like a movie projector uses a lens to shine light through it to project a film on a screen. This can happen at night while we are sleeping; it is called a *night vision* or a spiritual dream (see Matt. 1:20; 2:12-13).

This "film" can also be shown as a flash in our minds called an *inner vision.* This is how, when someone says, "Red fire engine," the image flashes into our minds (see Acts 5:1-4; 8:18-23). This type of vision (as with almost any vision) can come in prayer and worship or as we are talking with people or as we are simply going about our day. When this abstract flash comes into our minds and inside we sense, "Wait, why would that suddenly come into my mind?"—then it is time to pray about it, and inquire of God for clarity. The same should be done with every vision received.

The next stage of vision is the *open vision.* This is where the vision seems to be seen with our natural eyes, but it is not a natural thing we are seeing. It could become so intense that our spirits actually jump out to participate with it while our bodies become stationary. This is called a *trance* (see Acts 10:10-17).

The most vivid of all visions is when our physical bodies participate with the vision. This is called a *visitation* (see Acts 12:6-11). As we can tell from Peter's experience in Acts 12, sometimes it is difficult to tell while we are in the experience what kind of vision we are having! Even

Paul could not always tell right away (see 2 Cor. 12:1-4). The important thing is to have our imaginations set up properly to receive from the Lord. As we participate with this training, this will be possible.

THE WORD OF GOD: HOLY SPIRIT'S IMAGINATION

It is important to understand the difference between imagination and a vision from God, however. The Old Testament prophets constantly railed against those who called their own imaginations the "word of the Lord" (see Jer. 14:14; 23:16-17; Ezek. 13:1-8; Mic. 2:11). This is a dangerous line to cross because it sets up our own imaginations as God and can become the sin of idolatry! This is why it is important to keep the other parts of our souls cleansed with and obedient to the Word of God and to submit whatever vision we receive to God's Word and to prayer concerning it. A true vision from God will have an authority on it that cannot be manipulated like our imaginations can be. This doesn't mean that our imaginations aren't a powerful godly tool for the future, because *they are*. But it also doesn't mean that whatever we imagine is a direct message from God.

The guideline is this: We must train our imaginations to work in line with the Word of God first. If our imaginations are already working along those lines, it will be easier for the Spirit of God to help us out and "jump us up" to *His* level of imagination in our situations—which is not fantasy, but reality as He both sees and saw it. Think about this: *the Word of God both was and is the Holy Spirit's imagination!* Every event recorded in the Word of God has happened (and will happen) just as He imagined it would. That may be difficult to understand on our level, but it is still true. The Word of God trains our imaginations to "match the same frequency" as the Holy Spirit's imagination. We must just beware of trying to say with confidence what is on the channel before we even tune it correctly!

SPECTATOR OR DIRECTOR?

Here's one final note about training the imagination. Television and movies (also novels) are a powerful influence upon the imagination. They imprint images quite strongly upon the memory that will automatically cause the imagination to drift to them for fuel. When we are trying to get visions or revelation from God, images from television and movies can actually hijack and take over our imaginations, short-circuiting what God was trying to impart through our imaginations. It may be vital to actually abstain from these images in order to cleanse our minds with images from the Word of God. Movies and television programs are simply the products of other people's imaginations, and they can actually prevent us from developing our *own* imagination muscles.

If we insist upon watching a lot of television and movies, our imaginations will not become strong in a godly way. Our imaginations will become weak, very unfocused, and most likely polluted. Some television programs, films, and novels do have value for education and illustration, but the more of other ungodly people's imaginations we put into our minds, the more we will have to wash out in order to strengthen and use the imaginations that God gave us for our own lives.

Basically, the television moves the images for us. In training our imaginations, *we* must move the images because they will not be moved for us! In television, we are trained to be spectators. In life, we are trained to be actors. But with properly trained imaginations, we can become *directors*.

"IMAGINATION" REVIEW

1. The human imagination is the _____ tool for building into the realm of the spirit.

2. It is God's gift to _____ us places before we get there, to _____ things before we actually experience them, and to _____ things before we physically posses them.

3. When we _____ our imaginations, we _____ our future.

4. God created the imagination so that whatever the _____ _____, it can achieve.

5. The imagination is powerful, and its development does two things: it increases the _____ of our minds and it breaks _____ _____.

6. The Bible calls negative imaginations _____ (see 2 Cor. 10:4-5). They can _____ a person's life.

7. The power of the imagination does not belong to _____! When our imaginations are connected with God's Spirit, what happens in our minds will happen in _____. The key is to base it on promises or commands in the Word of God.

8. Second Corinthians 5:17 says we are new creations. But we need to let our _____ take hold of what this fully means! _____ and _____ work very closely together.

9. Discuss and describe some of the ways we can use our imaginations in our walk in the Spirit. (See pages 101-102.)

10. The more _____ our imaginations become, the more our spirits are released to welcome and experience God! *Describe some of the things you can imagine God doing and being toward you.*

11. Jesus used parables to create mental pictures that showed _____ realities (see Matt. 13:13-15). This helps us to use our imaginations so we can obey God where we previously had_____.

12. _____ (mental images) are _____ switches in the realm of the spirit.

13. The imagination brings things to life; it is a powerful _____ to access the power of God to heal, bless, and deliver (see Heb. 13:8; Acts 1:8; Heb. 11:1; Mark 11:22-23).

14. Discuss how the imagination can be used in ministering deliverance.

15. Before we do things for God, we must let our imaginations be our _____ _____. Then we see it beforehand in prayer. *How could using your imagination more in prayer forever change your prayer life?*

16. When God gives us pictures in our minds, then we must pray in the _____ and, in our imaginations, see ourselves accomplishing what He has shown us. We should use our imaginations only for *success,* never failure. *Why?*

17. The imagination-_____ connection is very strong. The imagination has a powerful impact upon our _____ abilities and potential to release them.

18. Matthew 5:28 shows that the power of the imagination is just as serious as the _____ act. God would never give more authority and ability to a _____ imagination than He would to a

_____ one! *Recall the things discussed in question 9. Do you take them as seriously as Matthew 5:28 describes?*

19. Imagine the issues in your life being _____ and _____ through God's promises. With the power of your imagination, you can take control of your past, present, and future.

20. The key to developing the imagination is to take the time to just _____ and _____. We must not just *do* something before our _____ has the chance to travel into that situation first and win the victory _____! *How do Second Corinthians 2:14 and Romans 8:37 relate to this important exercise?*

21. The following are several ways in which the Holy Spirit uses our imaginations:

    When we are sleeping it is a _____ _____.

    When it's a flash in our minds, it's called an _____ _____. When that happens we need to wait and pray about it and ask God for _____.

    The next vision is the _____ _____, which could also be called a _____ when our bodies are stationary, but our spirits are in the vision.

    The most vivid of all visions is called a _____.

    We may not be able to force these things to happen, but how do we set ourselves up to easily receive these revelations?

22. It's important to keep the other parts of our souls _____ and obedient to the Word of God and _____ whatever vision we receive to the Word and to _____ concerning it. A true vision from God will have an _____ that can't be

manipulated like our imaginations can. *How do we keep ourselves safe from crossing this line?* (See page 111.)

23. The Word of God was and is the _____ _____ imagination. So the Word trains our imaginations to match the same _____ as the _____ _____ imagination.

24. It may be _____ to _____ from other images like television and movies, which can prevent us from developing our own imagination muscles. *Why is this so?*

25. Television trains us to be _____; life will train us to be _____; but with properly trained imaginations, we can become _____.

26. (a) Plan *three times* in the upcoming week when, before doing a task, action, or activity, you don't do it right away, but you first stop, sit, and intently play out the situation in your mind. Be as vivid in your details as possible with your imagination! Imagine God moving with and through you in that task, and imagine your spirit being released in your voice, actions, and senses.

(b) After you have fully imagined all the aspects of that activity, then carry it out physically. Afterward, note the differences between the imagined action and your actual experience of that activity.

1) _____

2) _____

3) _____

(c) What happened that was good and exciting about your experiences?

(d) Rate yourself on the effectiveness of your imagination to play out the situation before it happened from 1-10.

(e) Afterward, replay the situation again with your imagination. Consider how you would do it differently or more effectively next time. (Then try the activity again and again; note your results!)

CHAPTER 8

THE WILL

This is the final part of the soul that we will discuss in our spirit life training. The human Will (I will capitalize the word *Will* to differentiate it from the future tense verb) is the strongest part of the human soul. It seems to stand silently in the far background behind all the soul's other colorful members, but it is the Will that has the final authority over what will happen in the human body, soul, and spirit.

REAL POWER = POWER TO *CHOOSE*

The Will is the gatekeeper of the spirit, soul, and body. It has the power to control what will or will not come in and out of the spirit. There was a time when the human Will was a struggling slave to the powers of sin and could never do what was right. It may be little known or preached, but the greatest power of salvation is the unchaining of the human Will.

> *For we know that the law is spiritual, but I am carnal, sold under sin. For what I am doing, I do not understand. For what I will to do, that I do not practice; but what I hate, that I do. If, then, I do what I will not to do, I agree with the law that it is good. But now, it is no longer I who do it, but sin that dwells in me. For I know that in me (that is, in my flesh)*

nothing good dwells; for to will is present with me, but how to perform what is good I do not find. For the good that I will to do, I do not do; but the evil I will not to do, that I practice. Now if I do what I will not to do, it is no longer I who do it, but sin that dwells in me. I find then a law, that evil is present with me, the one who wills to do good. For I delight in the law of God according to the inward man. But I see another law in my members, warring against the law of my mind, and bringing me into captivity to the law of sin which is in my members. O wretched man that I am! Who will deliver me from this body of death? I thank God—through Jesus Christ our Lord! So then, with the mind I myself serve the law of God, but with the flesh the law of sin. There is therefore now no condemnation to those who are in Christ Jesus, who do not walk according to the flesh, but according to the Spirit. For the law of the Spirit of life in Christ Jesus has made me free from the law of sin and death (Romans 7:14-8:2).

This passage tells us the torment of a Will that is bound to sin. It wants to be a good gatekeeper; it wants to do the right thing, but is bound to the desires of the flesh. Now, however, through the death of Jesus Christ for the sin of all mankind, the power of sin is broken. *Now* our Wills have regained the power to *choose*. It is God's greatest gift to humanity, and the devil's chief desire, that is, the control of the human Will. The devil knows he can no longer just grab control of a Christian's Will like he once could, so now his only power and strategy is to put influence and pressure upon the Will to do his pleasure through his seductive input to the other parts of the soul. (This is what the Bible calls *temptation.*) This is because it is the other parts of the soul that the Will listens to in order to make a quality decision. *But it doesn't always have to be that way!*

THE TRUE SUPERPOWER OF THE SOUL

In this spirit life training, we have hinted at this already, but we must now fully understand the unilateral power that the Will has over the rest of the soul and body.

Let me give an example: Let's say that you have just finished a nice meal at your mother's house. Just then—*ta daa*—out comes the birthday cake! Your eyes are filled with the sight of this wonderful delight to the taste buds, and your stomach automatically makes room for this new addition. Your imagination begins to look past the surface of the rich, creamy frosting to the soft, moist, melt-in-your-mouth butter cream cake insides. Your memory pulls a pleasant film from its files and starts playing the last time you had Mom's birthday cake. Yes, it was *your* birthday; look at all the happy faces of your friends laughing, having a good time, and there were the presents, and *wow* was that cake the *best*-tasting cake *ever!*

This triggers your emotions as a tear of joy begins to roll down your cheek at the memory. Yes, that was *so* much *fun!* Then Mom lovingly catches your eye as she sets down the cake in front of you and knowingly gives you her eager, delighted smile as she steps back. You know how much it means to your Mom when you enjoy her homemade cakes. You pick up the knife as your family and friends lean in closer (even holding out their plates). Your intelligence steps in for a moment to give its judgment. Yes, that will definitely blow your diet for today with those 30 grams of fat per serving, *but* that just means five to ten extra minutes on the treadmill tomorrow, right? So with those facts putting your conscience at ease and the smell—oh that yummy smell—filling your nostrils, you begin to hungrily stretch toward your prize.

But all of a sudden your Will steps in and says, *"No!* You will *not."* For a moment, everything freezes. Then all at once your body starts growling at you and the rest of your soul starts screaming, *Why? What is wrong with you?* And your body now gets to watch the disbelief and heartache of everyone else as your Will commands your body to put the knife down and push yourself away from the table. Congratulations. The war has just begun. But it doesn't matter how much growling and rebellion your body gives you or how much ammunition your imagination, intelligence, emotions, and memory will now try to fire at you; your Will has made the decision. And the rest of your frustrated body and soul will just have to line up with it whether they like it or not.

A SUCKLING BABY?

Now most of us who have just read that story did not like the outcome of that either. This is because most people's Wills could never make a decision like that. Most people's Wills are suckling babies to whatever the rest of their souls and bodies give to them and demand from them. They don't realize the latent power that the Will has to simply make a firm decision without needing any kind of majority vote from the rest of the soul and body. They have to obey *whatever the Will* decides. Our Wills have raw decision-making *power.* And we must know this: *Our lives are and always will be the result of the decisions we have made.* It is not the feelings we have felt, the situations that our bodies encounter, or the thoughts that our imaginations and intellects conjure up—but it is our *decisions* that ultimately form us.

TWO WORDS OUR WILLS LOVE

Our Wills feed on the two most basic words of the human language, *yes* and *no.* They are also the two most powerful words in the human language. Our Wills use the freedom God gave them to use these two words to determine the boundaries of both God and the devil in our lives! The more we say *yes* to God, the more He can do through and with our lives. The more we say *no* to God, the less access He has to direct and help us in our lives. God gave humankind a free human Will that He will not violate. From the beginning of creation, that was the basis of all human authority on Earth. When humankind sinned, it was because humankind yielded control of the human Will to obey the devil. This, in effect, gave the devil authority on Earth, because he could now work his will through the Will of humankind.

And overall, people became the puppets and the devil became the puppet master. There were a few (Moses, Joshua, Samuel, David, and so forth) who took back their Wills and submitted them once more to God, but as a general rule, people's Wills were now under the dominion of the devil. But after Jesus came, broke the devil's influence over His own Will, died for the disobedience of the rest of the sinful choices by the Wills of humankind, and rose from the dead—*He gave authority back to humankind's Will*. But there was a catch. It is only through faith in Jesus and abiding in Him that the Will of humankind overcomes the devil's will. *"Therefore submit* [your Will] *to God. Resist the devil* [with your Will] *and he will flee from you"* (James 4:7).

When we have submitted our Wills to God and we say *no* to the devil concerning our lives, it produces a line and law in the spirit that he cannot cross! But if we don't say *no* to the devil in a certain area of our lives (or even worse, say *yes* to him), that gives him access into that area of our lives. Our Will's food is through the forceful use of the words *yes* and *no* in our lives. We teach our children how to use these words very early in life. But have we forgotten the force they have for the rest of our lives?

Say them: "Yes!" "No!" Now keep practicing until you can feel your Will rising up on the inside of you with strength. The life changes produced by strengthening your Will could dramatically alter your present circumstances. The funny thing is that people will say, "Wow, your personality has really changed!" Realize that the people who have grown used to controlling you will not like the "new" you. But the truth is that the *real* you is beginning to rise up and take charge of your life.

LAZY, PASSIVE, AND EVENTUALLY USELESS WILL

Let me back up and give some details about the Will as it would be used in an ungodly manner. First of all, it will be *lazy*. It has no zeal or passion and becomes very passive to people and circumstances that are around it. Very few people have personal issues with these kinds of people when they first meet them (except when they are their employees) because they are so easygoing and they don't want to cause trouble. But eventually they become useless like the salt Jesus talks about in Luke 14:34-35. They don't make any difference in life; their Wills are passive and indecisive. They are controlled by circumstances and are double-minded. Their Wills can be easily manipulated by other parts of the soul (or other people's souls) and not by committed decisions. They rely on other people's opinions continually and are generally full of doubt.

FIGHTING FOR THE WRONG SIDE

The other path that an ungodly Will can take is to be strongly rebellious. This kind of Will is strong, but is strong about the wrong things! This kind of Will can take any wrong information from the intelligence, imagination, memory, and *especially the emotions*, and just take it to the extreme. By whatever truth God seeks to bring conviction about, this kind of Will protects the other parts of the soul (or so it thinks) by refusing to admit that the information it received (from the other parts of the soul) was wrong. This kind of Will motivates the other parts of the soul to think, imagine, remember, or feel whatever they can to justify themselves and strengthen their position. This rebellious Will feeds off of the contaminations of the other parts of the soul, making strong decisions and motivating actions contrary to the Word of God.

While the first kind of ungodly Will is like a ship on the sea without a sail, the second kind of ungodly Will is like a blind driver in a four-wheel drive truck who is motivated to get somewhere, but will run over anything and anyone in the way to get there. He may feel a bump or two and decide to shift into a higher gear, knowing that this *must* be the way and wonders why his truck is no longer functioning after it hits a wall or flips over. For this kind of ungodly Will, we can only pray that pain will be an effective wake-up call (see Heb. 12:5-11).

HOW TO BREAK THE DEVIL'S WILL

We *should* have strong Wills. But according to James 4:7-8, it is only when we strongly align our Wills with God's Will that we will have power to break the devil's Will! He does have a Will, but it is against God's Will.

Here's an example. Let's say the devil wants to keep you in poverty all your life. That is the devil's Will; he comes to steal, kill, and destroy (see John 10:10). But the Will of God is that you have life more abundantly and that you be in health and prosper (see John 10:10; 3 John 2). But the question is, what do *you* want? If you believe your present circumstances and your past failures, the devil's Will has won. Poverty is now your future.

But once you renew your soul by establishing in your memory, intelligence, imagination, and emotions that God wants you to prosper and you start understanding the character, integrity, creativity, generosity, and faith of a prosperous person as recorded in God's Word, your Will can start aligning itself with God's Will for prosperity. It is then—every day—you start backing the devil up and out of your life. His Will starts to bend, break, and snap under the pressure of your Will aligned with God's Will.

GOD'S WILL ALWAYS JUST HAPPENS?

The basic puzzlement of humankind concerning God's Will is this: If God is an Almighty God, He can do whatever He wants to do, right? So if this is so, whatever happens must be God's Will, right? Wrong. This is a misunderstanding of the fact that God *will not* violate people's Wills about their personal lives. If people want to go to hell, fine. God will not stop them. If people want to live in sickness and poverty, fine. God will not stop them. It's too bad that these things are *not* what God wants, but are *what the devil wants* for people, *but people must make the choice about what **they** really want!* The devil will do everything he can to influence people to do what he wants them to do, but God has clearly given His Word on what His Will is concerning these things and more! If we will learn of this and align our Wills firmly to say *yes* to His Will and *no* to the devil's Will, that's it. Victory is in our hands. This is the kind of salvation that God is looking for—not just forgiving the past, but saving our Wills from the devil's present desires for us!

ALIGNMENT: AN INNER RESPONSE TO GOD

This salvation is through aligning our Wills with God's Will.

*Therefore, my beloved, as you have always obeyed, not as in my presence only, but now much more in my absence, work out your own salvation with fear and trembling; for it is God who **works in you** both to **will** and to **do** for His good pleasure* (Philippians 2:12-13).

So this is a fantastic part of spirit life training—letting God's Spirit transform and align *everything* in our souls with God's Will. He is not just standing around waiting for us to "get with the program." He is working *in* and *with* us to do what He wants, as we just say *yes* to however He wants to work on the inside of us! Spirit life growth in the Will becomes more of a response to His leadings on the inside than it is an effort through trial and error to find out what He wants us to do. We will talk more about how to receive and respond to these leadings later. Right now, just know that as we submit our Wills to Him, He forms our Wills to do His Will! If we can achieve this, we can achieve anything.

WHAT WE ARE REALLY FIGHTING FOR

Think of it—if we are working with God, who could possibly stop us? This is why praying for God's Will to be established in our Wills should be the main objective of all our praying!

> *Epaphras, who is one of you, a bondservant of Christ greets you, always laboring fervently for you in prayers, that you may stand perfect and complete in all the will of God* (Colossians 4:12).

This man knew that the alignment of the human Will with the Will of God was the key to unstoppable victory. Jesus also wrestled for this objective in prayer (see Luke 22:40-44). So many people know the Lord's Prayer; what was the first thing that Jesus taught humans to ask for? *"Your kingdom come, **Your Will be done on earth** as it is in heaven"* (Matt. 6:10). The basic fact is: No one can fight God's Will and win. But God needs some willing pray-ers who will participate and let their Wills be strongly aligned to how God is poised to move on this planet.

We must not fall for the lie, "Oh, if God wants it to happen, it will just happen; God is sovereign." No; it does not work that way. The testimony of the Scripture from Genesis to Revelation is that God's participation with the human Will is His chief desire. He has sovereignly chosen to let people know His written Will and has given people the choice to release it through their faith and actions. *The more strongly people's Wills are aligned with God's Will, the more strongly God's Will is released to actually occur.* This should give us a powerful clue regarding what *attitude* we should have when we pray (see Luke 11:2-13). *We must keep pounding "the door" in prayer, violently and persistently,* **until His Will manifests** *in our lives.* That doesn't offend Him at all! The more strongly our Wills demand His Will, the more He is pleased. He knows we are pressing in to be more like Him!

"I WILL..."

How do we strengthen our Wills? We already talked about one way—through forcefully using the words *yes* and *no*. Hopefully we have all already taken the time to do that. Another way mirrors the exercise for the emotions. It is through the bold "I *will*..." declarations of the Word of God. This is quite powerful. We boldly declare, "I *will* love the Lord my God with all my heart, soul, mind, and strength" (see Mark 12:30). "I *will* bless the Lord at all times, and His praise *shall* continually be in my mouth" (see Ps. 34:1). "I *will* be strong in the Lord and in the power of His might" (see Eph. 6:10). In our memorization exercises, we can add this exercise, using those same Scriptures to boost our Will's strength as well.

"THE WILL" REVIEW

1. The human _____ is the strongest part of the human soul and has the _____ _____ of what happens in the human body, soul, and spirit.

2. The Will is the _____ of the spirit, soul, and body. The greatest power of salvation is the _____ of the human Will (see Rom. 7:14-8:2).

3. The _____ of the human Will is God's greatest gift to people and the _____ chief desire.

4. The devil's strategy is to put _____ and _____ upon the Will. This is what the Bible calls _____.

5. Most people's Wills are _____ _____ to whatever the rest of their souls and bodies give to them and demand from them. The Will has to _____ make a firm decision without needing any kind of majority vote from the rest of the soul and body. They _____ whatever the Will decides.

6. Our lives are and always will be the _____ of the _____ we have made.

7. The two most powerful words in the human language are _____ and _____. Our _____ use these two words to determine the boundaries of both God and the devil in our lives.

8. After Jesus came and broke the power of the devil's influence over His own Will, He gave _____ back to humankind's Will.

However, it is only through faith in Jesus and abiding in God's Will that we overcome the devil's Will (see James 4:7-8). We have the power to break the devil's Will when we _____ our Wills with God's.

9. When we have submitted our Wills to God and we say *no* to the devil, it produces a _____ and a _____ in the spirit that he cannot cross. Our Will's food is through the forceful use of _____ and _____.

10. Ungodly Wills are _____ and _____. When the Will is in this state, the soul will continually be able to feed it wrong information, especially the _____!

11. God will not _____ people's Wills about their personal lives. The kind of salvation God is looking for is not just forgiving the past, but _____ our Wills from the devil's desires for us! People must make the choice!

12. Read Philippians 2:12-13. People can allow God's _____ to transform and align _____ in their souls with God's Will.

13. Colossians 4:12 and Matthew 6:10 tell us that God's _____ _____ with the human Will is His chief desire.

14. The more strongly people's Wills are aligned with God's Will, the more strongly God's Will is released to occur. Our _____ should be to boldly persist in prayer until His Will _____ in our lives.

15. Our Wills get stronger by using the words _____ and _____ and through the bold use of the words _____ _____!

Practice saying these words boldly until you feel strong and solid on the inside with their use.

Your goal during the coming week is to find three (or more) situations like the one on page 121 and exercise your Will to push against all the other forces of your soul and body to complete that action. (Do make sure it is scriptural and profitable first, however.) Afterward, note below what happens to your attitude and strength on the inside.

1) _____

_____

_____

_____

2) _____

_____

_____

_____

3) _____

_____

_____

_____

CHAPTER 9

PUTTING IT ALL TOGETHER

BODYBUILDING FOR THE SOUL

I have done my best to split apart the different areas of the soul in order to train each one of them more fully and individually. In a very real way, it is similar to physical exercise. Physical sports and calisthenics use a lot of different muscles, and through them people can become physically fit, healthy, and strong. However, in these general exercises, many muscles are worked at the same time, and because of this, there is not a great increase in strength like there would be in weightlifting or bodybuilding. In weight-training activities, each muscle group is focused on individually, and because of this, strength comes more easily to each individual muscle group, which in turn causes the whole body to increase in strength.

This is like what I have done here in the separation of the soulish elements of emotion, intellect, memory, imagination, and Will. Although in practice each will use and affect the other parts of the soul (and the exercises are not so foreign if we have been involved with Christian disciplines for any length of time), the focus we apply to each one will build each part up individually and, in so doing, will produce a collectively healthy and powerful soul through which the spirit can be released easily.

Here's a well-known example of a fully-trained soul that produces miraculous results—the story of David and Goliath in First Samuel 17. In this example, I want to show how each part of David's soul was strongly aligned to God and His Word in order for this victory to be obtained.

The Emotions

> *Then David spoke to the men who stood by him, saying, "What shall be done for the man who kills this Philistine and takes away the reproach from Israel? For who is this uncircumcised Philistine, that he should defy the armies of the living God?"* (1 Samuel 17:26)

From reading this, we can hear the anger, indignation, and contempt in David's response to this threat. How different these emotions were from the fear that everyone else felt in the face of Goliath! David was upset that anyone would dare to intimidate God's own people! When David's brother tried to pull rank on him and condemn him down to the level of intimidation that everyone else had, David responded with another godly emotion—*boldness.* *"And David said, 'What have I done now? Is there not a cause?'"* (1 Sam. 17:29). His boldness was rooted in the righteous *cause* of standing for God and for His people's honor.

The Will

> *"Then David said to Saul, 'Let no man's heart fail because of him; your servant will go and fight this Philistine'"* (1 Sam. 17:32). While everyone else was standing around for 40 days and listening in fear to this giant, David made a *decision.* No one else would make a decision, but David used his words to make a clear choice: *"I will go and fight."*

The Memory

> *And Saul said to David, "You are not able to go against this Philistine to fight with him; for you are a youth, and he a man of war from his youth." But David said to Saul, "Your servant used to keep his father's sheep, and when a lion or a bear came and took a lamb out of the flock, I went out after it and struck it, and delivered the lamb from its mouth; and when it arose against me, I caught it by its beard, and struck and killed it. Your servant has killed both lion and bear; and this uncircumcised Philistine will be like one of them, seeing he has defied the armies of the living God"* (1 Samuel 17:33-36).

David's memory of past victories gave him the courage to face the upcoming battle. To him, the enemy may have been different, but in his mind, the situations were so similar that he really felt he could replay the same past outcome with this present challenge. Those past victories were imprinted so strongly in his memory—and thank God that they were! Those memories became momentum-building agents to cause him to run to the battle to defeat an enemy who seemed impossible to defeat. (How strongly are *your* past victories over temptation or the devil's attack imprinted in *your* memory? It is *not* humility to disregard and forget them! That is simply ungrateful mental laziness. Recall and rejoice in them continually!)

The Intellect

> *So Saul clothed David with his armor, and he put a bronze helmet on his head; he also clothed him with a coat of mail. David fastened his sword to his armor and he tried to walk, for he had not tested them. And David said to Saul, "I cannot walk with these, for I have not tested them." So David took them off* (1 Samuel 17:38-39).

David knew that these weapons would not be effective for him because he had no experience with them. He had some knowledge of warfare (see 1 Sam. 16:18) and understood that he shouldn't go into a dangerous combat situation with gear that he was not familiar with! He considered these facts and reasoned that the weapons he knew *how* to use would be enough with God on his side. He reasoned that, since God had helped him against the lion and the bear with these weapons, He would also help him against the Philistine with these weapons. He knew that if he was going to fight now, this was his only option!

The Imagination

And when the Philistine looked about and saw David, he disdained him; for he was only a youth, ruddy and good-looking. So the Philistine said to David, "Am I a dog, that you come to me with sticks?" And the Philistine cursed David by his gods. And the Philistine said to David, "Come to me, and I will give your flesh to the birds of the air and the beasts of the field!" Then David said to the Philistine, "You come to me with a sword, with a spear, and with a javelin. But I come to you in the name of the Lord of hosts, the God of the armies of Israel, whom you have defied. This day the Lord will deliver you into my hand, and I will strike you and take your head from you. And this day I will give the carcasses of the camp of the Philistines to the birds of the air and the wild beasts of the earth, that all the earth may know that there is a God in Israel. Then all this assembly shall know that the Lord does not save with sword and spear; for the battle is the Lord's and He will give you into our hands" (1 Samuel 17:42-47).

This is an amazing display of imagination on David's part. Everything he saw in the natural was contrary to what he saw in his mind, but he still saw it so vividly and spoke it boldly. (You *must* see it vividly if you are going to speak it boldly!)

Goliath was bigger on the outside, but his imagination was smaller on the inside! He imagined killing David and then the birds and beasts eating him. David did better than that; he imagined the *whole army* of the Philistines dead and the birds and the beasts feeding on the whole lot of them! Look at how detailed and methodical David's words were concerning his upcoming victory. He did not just say he was going to "do his best, and God will do the rest." He imagined this giant being struck dead. He imagined that Goliath's head would be chopped off. David didn't even have a sword to do that with—*yet!* But he knew that is how the battle would be settled in his eyes.

The battle does not belong to the bigger warrior, but the bigger imagination on the inside of the warrior. Like Oral Roberts has said, "If you can see the invisible, you can do the impossible."[1] (See Hebrews 11:24-27.) David's imagination saw a bigger giant than Goliath; he saw the invisible God, and David's imagination caused his emotions to feel the fury of Jehovah at how this giant has mocked His name and His people. David's imagination locked him into a zone where God and David were now acting as one. David's imagination reversed the situation to where it was not David who was in trouble any longer; it was the giant who was now in trouble.

ANATOMY OF A MIRACLE

Now, look at the perfect alignment of David's soul to the Spirit of God. As was mentioned earlier, the goal of the soul is to be unlocked like a combination lock—where all the numbers are lined up so precisely that the Spirit of God can be released through our beings in a moment's notice. David's soul was in such an alignment. Because of this, as soon as David released these words from his spirit (picture this in slow motion), the Spirit of God shot through his soul and flooded his body with such an energy that he bolted off running straight at the giant. His arms were flooded with that same strength, and he didn't miss a beat as he reached into his pouch, pulled out a rock, set it in the sling, whipped it around, and released it with pinpoint accuracy straight to the bull's-eye—the forehead of Goliath.

People try to say that David hit a spot where Goliath's helmet was not protecting him; I can't say that for sure. But I do know that there had to be a force on that rock that was more than natural. The forehead part of the skull is quite tough, and on a giant, it would have to be thicker than on a normal human. Now to crack a skull with a rock is one thing, but to totally pierce and penetrate the forefront of a skull with a rock like a bullet seems hardly possible. If people knew that rocks from shepherd's slings could do that kind of damage easily, why weren't they used in battle more often?

Both sides were stunned; this is why no one believed the giant was dead until the head was chopped off. The energy that propelled that rock started in the realm of the Spirit of God. It was released into David's spirit, gained momentum through David's perfectly aligned soul, flooded into his body, overflowed through his hand, and was finally released into that same stone that was propelled at such a force to pierce the giant's skull (helmet or no helmet).

It's the same technology that Paul used when handkerchiefs were taken from his body to heal the sick and cast out devils in Acts 19:11-12. There is no inherent power in a cotton handkerchief to do those things, just like there is no inherent power in a rock to kill a giant in that manner. But when the body is disciplined and the soul is perfectly aligned—emotions, intellect, memory, imagination and will—to the spirit, then there is nothing to stop the power of God flowing out from the spirit into the body to any object to do a supernatural work! Remember Moses' rod, Elijah's mantle, and Elisha's bones (see Exod. 7:14-21;

2 Kings 2:8; 2 Kings 13:21); even Jesus used objects to transmit the power of God, like spit, mud, His clothes, water, fish, and loaves of bread (see Mark 8:23; John 9:6; Mark 5:27-30; John 2:6-10; Matt. 14:16-21).

As we train ourselves in each of the exercises for the individual parts of the soul to line up with God's Spirit and His Word, we will be able to experience more of the life of the Spirit flowing through us on a daily basis. Yes, it can be a battleground. But like David, our souls can also be a victory platform!

ENDNOTE

1. Oral Roberts, *Still Doing the Impossible: When You See the Invisible, You Can Do the Impossible* (Shippensburg, PA: Destiny Image Publishers, 2002), 6.

"PUTTING IT ALL TOGETHER" REVIEW

1. The _____ we apply to the disciplines we've discussed (and exercised) will produce a healthy, powerful _____ through which the _____ can be released easily.

2. David's _____ produced _____, which was rooted in the cause of standing for God's people.

3. David made a _____ which was "___ _____ go out and fight!"

4. We need to _____ and _____ in our past victories.

5. David considered the _____ and reasoned that the _____ he knew *how* to use would be _____ *with God on his side.*

6. In order to _____ our decisions boldly, we must first see them _____ in our imaginations.

7. "If you can see the _____ you can do the _____," according to Oral Roberts.

8. David's energy started in the _____ of the _____.

9. When the _____ is disciplined and the _____ is perfectly aligned to the _____, there is nothing that can stop the _____ of God.

10. Our souls can be _____ _____!

11. Think and discuss other situations in which you or someone else put the "total package" of the soul together. This week your goal is

to perform three complete situations in which each part of you is fully engaged in the activity. Use what you have learned and experienced from past exercises and then put it into full use on at least three separate occasions this week. (Have a competition to see who can have the most situations!) It may be something you have dealt with in some of the previous exercises as well. Note the results this time. What part of you needs to be worked on more? It should become even more apparent after this exercise.

Situation #1:

_____

_____

_____

_____

Situation #2:

_____

_____

_____

_____

Situation #3:

_____

_____

_____

_____

CHAPTER 10

THE SPIRIT—"THE REAL YOU"

This part of us is, again, the *real* us. For teaching purposes, I will continue to refer to the spirit part of us as a third party, but in reality, *it is who we are.*

This is so vital to understand. When we really understand it, we will automatically start putting the spirit part of us first, rather than letting it compete and be confused in rank with our souls and bodies. As we will see, when we put *our spirits* first, decisions become easier. First, it is because our power is greater to be able to do the Will of God, and second, it is because *our priorities* are clearer! (Please note that, here and elsewhere, the plural term *our spirits* is used to indicate one spirit in each of us, not multiple spirits in any one individual.)

There are distinct reasons in the Bible for why the spirit part of us must be first.

> *For to me, to live is Christ, and to die is gain. But if I live on in the flesh, this will mean fruit from my labor; yet what I shall choose I cannot tell. For I am hard-pressed between the two, having a desire to depart and be with Christ, which is far better. Nevertheless to remain in the flesh is more needful for you* (Philippians 1:21-24).

Paul knew the difference between who he (his spirit) was and what his flesh was. He was able to feel the pull of his spirit for Christ and also know what kind of purpose his spirit had in the earth in Christ! Because he knew the power of his spirit to impact the earth, he could use the authority in his spirit to choose to remain on earth and continue to bear fruit for the Kingdom of God. Because his spirit was first, he knew his priorities.

A THOUSAND TIMES BIGGER ON THE INSIDE

Paul wrote, *"Therefore we do not lose heart. Even though our outward man is perishing, yet the inward man is being renewed day by day"* (2 Cor. 4:16). The fact of life is that the body does get older and will eventually die. However, that is not true concerning the spirit within a person. The spirit just keeps getting stronger and stronger as it is released more and more.

Smith Wigglesworth had a great saying, *"In me is working a power stronger than every other power...The life that is in me is a thousand times bigger than I am outside."*[1] He was not ashamed of the fact that on the inside of his average build Englishman's body, he had a hulking, muscle-bound, juggernaut spirit that could snatch, pull down, and tear up ancient demonic princes like wet tissue paper.

But the same is true for anyone who believes this promise: *"You are of God, little children, and have overcome them, because He who is in you is greater than he who is in the world"* (1 John 4:4).

IS OUR TREASURE BURIED?

The Scriptures give this amazing statement in Second Corinthians 4:7: *"But we have this treasure in earthen vessels, that the excellence of the power may be of God and not of us."* We know that our bodies are made from the dust of the earth (see Gen. 2:7). That is the earthen vessel, but what is the treasure that displays the excellence of the power of God? It is our spirit. It is a treasure that is, in a sense, buried in our vessels of earth! The tragedy is that most people keep it buried their entire lives.

It's like the parable Jesus told of the talents that the master entrusted to his servants. Some exposed and invested their talents to increase them, but one chose to bury it until the master returned. The master strongly condemned that servant, calling him lazy and wicked (see Matt. 25:25-27). However, he didn't *lose* his talent; he just didn't *use* his talent!

We are often envious of spiritual "giants" of the faith and say, "Well, God chose them for a special work, and they were endowed with special gifts and callings." Each person *is* special, each person *does* have a special calling, and we have *all* been given a treasure that is worth more than 10 million dollars—it is the spirit part of us! Will we keep it buried? Or will we use it to release God into the earth?

WE ALREADY HAVE WHAT WE NEED

God did not leave us unequipped. We're just like the computer slogan, which says, "It's all inside." Victory is inside. Health is inside. Wisdom is inside. Love is inside. Prosperity is inside. Everything we need to get through life victoriously is already inside. Because *God is inside!* This is our secret weapon, our hidden power switch. This is our true strength. No matter what we may look like on the inside, we do not judge ourselves because of what our flesh looks like (see 2 Cor. 5:16-17), but based on the Christ who is manifesting through our flesh through the release of the strength of our spirits.

This is what Paul prayed for the believers in Ephesians 3:16, *"That He would grant you, according to the riches of His glory, to be strengthened with might through His Spirit in the inner man."* He wanted every believer's spirit to be strong, to break through the earthen vessels and touch others around them! This is what Jesus was known for—long before He started His teaching, healing, and delivering ministry! *"And the Child grew and became strong in spirit, filled **with wisdom; and the grace of God was upon Him"** (Luke 2:40). This was when He was under 12 years old! How much more should we expect to be known for our strength of spirit early in our spiritual growth! It is a priority in God's eyes.

When you put your spirit first, you put your true strength first, and you get more done faster!

THE AUTHORITY OF OUR SPIRIT

Another reason that the spirit should be put in ascendancy over the soul and the body is that our spirits have an authority in the earth that far outranks any other position we may possess naturally. From president, to CEO, to general…our spirits have authority in realms that control even these high-ranking natural positions!

> *Blessed be the God and Father of our Lord Jesus Christ, who has blessed us with every spiritual blessing in the heavenly places in Christ…(By grace you have been saved), and* [He] *raised us up together and made us sit together in heavenly places in Christ Jesus* (Ephesians 1:3; 2:5b-6).

When we can come into situations with the authority of our position in Christ Jesus, we can walk confidently knowing that we have the ability to produce environments where God is going to root out evil and start something good. Why is voting for the right rulers important? Rulers have the authority to produce laws that can limit lawlessness and stimulate pro-ductivity in an environment—or vice versa! So they have power to do good or do evil or *do nothing*! The last choice is sad, but it is the choice that many Christians make with the authority that has been given to them in their spirits! We *can* change an environment and make it productive for God because of the authority given to us as we put our spirits *first*.

APPEARANCES CAN BE DECEIVING

Some people think that a strong body equals a strong spirit. We should know by now that this is a false assumption. A bodybuilder who has no development in his spirit is weak compared to the 90-year-old grandmother whose spirit is strong enough to shift natural and spiritual circumstances through her prayers and words alone. Some people may be strong enough to pick up 500 pounds of weight, but are they strong enough to pick up a city spiritually? Are they strong enough to lift off the spirit of death from a cancer victim? There are circumstances in which even the strongest people feel helpless. But when people's spirits are strong enough, there is no circumstance where they need to feel helpless.

Some people think that a strong personality equals a strong spirit. That is not necessarily true, either. A strong personality usually means a strong soul, but a strong spirit is different. A strong spirit has the ability to stand against evil forces, yet stay humble before God. It stands strong in the things that are right, but it also has the ability to impact the depths of people's hearts in a supernatural way. This is because the spirit is the eternal part of us. What is done by the flesh won't last. What is done by the soul won't last. It is only the strong spirit that can build something that touches the eternal and that will leave its mark for a lifetime and beyond.

SIGNS OF A STRONG SPIRIT

There are signs of a strong spirit, some of which are similar to the characteristics of a strong personality. A strong spirit has a voice of authority. This is sometimes loud, but always decisive. A strong spirit is determined to see God's will come to pass. A strong spirit has a buoyant joy about it, but also a peace that stabilizes the environment around it. A strong spirit has an ability to influence people and initiate action. But a strong spirit is also influenced easily by intangible factors. It has an internal radar that picks up small signals in the character of circumstances, people, and other influences and makes decisions based on the consequences of truth rather than the appearance of things.

FEEDING OUR SPIRITS' NEEDS

When we first talked about our three parts, we talked about the needs of the spirit, the soul, and the body. Each one has needs and desires. Basically, whatever need or desire we choose to feed will grow stronger. Whatever need or desire we do not feed will grow weaker.

The objective is to feed each part of our beings based on *priorities*. We don't neglect any part that God gave us, but we still must recognize that the spirit is the priority if we are to have harmony and success in our lives with God. When we are born again, our spirits are made brand new. They are infused with the life of God. In a sense, they grow stronger through prayer, the Word, and worshiping God. As we read earlier in Ephesians 3:16, the spirit in each of us *can* get stronger. That is both a gift we ask for and a development that we *choose* to work on! So everything that we will be talking about in this chapter about the spirit is about feeding and developing the strength of it.

OUR COMMUNICATION DEVICE

In our modern times, there are so many ways in which communication occurs. Cell phone, fax, email, text message, Bluetooth, Wi-Fi, instant messenger, Webcams, answering machine, Facebook,

Twitter—there are so many devices because communication is the life-blood of relationships and commerce.

Our healthy relationship with God is the same way; it is built upon communication. Just as in the natural world, there are many communication devices and just as many ways to miscommunicate! The cell phone may be off, the email system may be down, the fax may not go through, the text message may be delayed—it has happened to all of us.

God can try to communicate with us in so many ways, but there is *one* "communication device" that must be on or none of the messages God tries to give us will ever get to us: it is the spirit part of us. That is how we talk to Him; that is how we love Him; that is how we worship Him; that is how we listen to Him. It is so important to know this. If our spirit isn't activated, miscommunication *will* occur.

GOD'S METHODS OF COMMUNICATION

People always want God to do something dramatic to communicate with them. In the Old Testament, that was how God had to communicate with people. He had to set a bush on fire for Moses. He had to send angels to Joshua. He had to send prophets for the nations. He had to answer by fire, thunder, booming voices from Heaven, and so forth. This sounds spectacular, but it really wasn't effective. People got so caught up in the method that they sometimes missed the message. So God came down in the form of Jesus Christ—the ultimate form of communication—the Word becoming flesh. This was the most effective way so far, but it wasn't the end. Jesus Himself told the next step in God's master communication upgrade.

> *Nevertheless I tell you the truth. It is to your advantage that I go away; for if I do not go away, the Helper will not come to you; but if I depart, I will send Him to you....I still have many*

things to say to you, but you cannot bear them now. However, when He, the Spirit of truth, has come, He will guide you into all truth; for He will not speak on His own authority, but whatever He hears He will speak; and He will tell you things to come (John 16:7,12-13).

Jesus had to die on a cross to pay for the spiritual death that had come to every human being's spirit through sin. After He was raised from the dead, He gave the right to humankind to be spiritually reborn, enabling each person's spirit to come back to life and communicate with God the Father. When we receive the Lord Jesus Christ as Savior, we give Him the right to send the Holy Spirit into our hearts, but not to be quiet. Rather, *"...you received the Spirit of adoption by whom we cry out 'Abba, Father.' The Spirit Himself bears witness with our spirit that we are children of God..."* (Rom. 8:15-16).

It is an upgrade of our spirits to receive the Holy Spirit, by which we can freely communicate with God. This is the new and better way of communication that the Old Testament believers did not have access to like we do in the New Testament. So when we ask God to do something dramatic like "write me a message in the sky" or "make my Alpha-Bits divinely come out into my bowl to spell that You love me," what we are saying is that we need to be born again. After we are born again, God communicates to us through the reborn spirit; it is His communication device with us directly.

> *This is the covenant that I will make with them after those days, says the Lord: I will put My laws into their hearts, and in their minds I will write them* (Hebrews 10:16).

In this passage, *heart* means the spirit part of us which can now upload those messages into our minds (souls). God is not fleshly or soulish; He is a Spirit and will communicate with us starting on that level.

UPGRADING OUR CONNECTION SPEED

Of course, God can still do all those things He did in the Old Testament, but the Word declares that they are no longer His chosen methods of communicating with His people. An example is like this: Imagine I want to talk with you. I come over to your house and start talking to the house. Are you the house? No. You live *in* the house. So you invite me in, and I start walking throughout the house talking to the furniture, appliances, clothes closets, pets, and so forth. Are those things you? No, those may be *an expression* of you, but those things are not you! I talk to you when I am face-to-face with you.

God wants to communicate directly to us (via the spirit within us), not to our houses (our bodies/flesh/natural realm) or our "stuff" (our souls/feelings). This is one of the biggest purposes of our spirits—to receive communication from God.

Our spirits are supposed to be like the Internet connection (in a manner of speaking) that is on 24 hours a day. You can receive downloads from God anytime—in the form of words, pictures, visions, dreams, spiritual deposits of strength, wisdom, healing, miracles, and so forth. God is communicating these things to us, to our spirits, all the time.

> But as it is written: *"Eye has not seen, nor ear heard, nor have entered into the heart of man the things which God has prepared for those who love Him." **But God has revealed them to us through His Spirit.** For the Spirit searches all things, yes, the deep things of God.... Now we have received, not the spirit of the world, but the Spirit who is from God, that we might know the things that have been freely given to us by God* (1 Corinthians 2:9-10,12).

If we are operating in faith, believing that this Scripture is so, we can start using these things that have been downloaded to us!

DIVINE DOWNLOADS

To continue with the computer analogy, these downloads come in the form of zip files. The messages can be downloaded quickly, but our souls must open them to see what manner of download they are and how they can be used. But if we don't believe that our spirits can receive from God at anytime, or if we think the Holy Spirit doesn't have a very good "anti-virus software system," and instead we believe that demons are actually putting these downloads through instead of God—we won't open them. We will just delete these gifts right away, missing the blessings of the things God has prepared for us. This is why, after teaching on prayer, Jesus speaks right away about expecting and accepting good gifts from God.

> If a son asks for bread from any father among you, will he give him a stone? Or if he asks for a fish, will he give him a serpent instead of a fish? Or if he asks for an egg, will he offer him a scorpion? If you then, being evil, know how to give good gifts to your children, how much more will your heavenly Father give the Holy Spirit to those who ask Him? (Luke 11:11-13)

As long as the combination is unlocked and aligned to the Word, everything we download can be trusted as being *good* and needful, if not for ourselves, then for someone else around us. Living life with a "dial-up modem" spirit is going to be too slow to be effective in these times. If we have to stop, pray, dial up the combination, wait, and hope the connection is established before we can really help and be helped, it takes too long. Just like in the natural, with a dial-up modem some things take too long to download. God will not download some things until a faster-speed connection is hooked up continually. It is time to upgrade!

BEWARE: OUR SEARCH ENGINES

Now, while we are hooked up at this higher-speed connection, we can't abuse it! If we are desiring after the works of the flesh, such as those listed in Galatians 5:19-21, the Holy Spirit anti-virus warning *will* alert us of the danger through our consciences. But if we insist on playing around with the works of the flesh, some things will be downloaded that can mess up our hard drives—both the soul and the spirit—as well as our flesh.

> *Therefore, having these promises, beloved, let us cleanse ourselves from all filthiness of the flesh and spirit, perfecting holiness in the fear of God* (2 Corinthians 7:1).

As a reminder, *both Galatians and Second Corinthians were written to born-again, Spirit-filled Christians.* Let's keep our spirit connections purely focused on God and His purposes; then every download we get will be pure and useful to ourselves and others.

SPIRITUAL = SPOOKY?

This leads us to another important point. Some people think that living a spiritual life means that no one will understand us (which is true to a point, according to First Corinthians 2:14-16). They think we must live in caves, eat only bread and water, have a strange look in our eyes when we talk with people, are overly serious all the time, and *never laugh or have fun.* Now, we are to be sober-minded and alert according to First Peter 5:8, but we must be able to relate with people. Jesus was our example as the most spiritual person to walk the earth. Yet He could relate to children, businessmen, soldiers, prostitutes, mothers, fishermen, and so forth; He even had *friends.* There were times where He was misunderstood, but the key was that

He did not reject people. He gave them the *way,* the *truth,* and the *life* (see John 14:6).

ACCUSED OF "BEING RELIGIOUS"

One secret fear many Christians have is that someone will call them "religious." Many years ago, this was actually a compliment of respect, but in modern times, the term seems to have changed in meaning.

In modern times, the term *religious* means that people are too into the duties of religion to have time for fun and enjoyment with other people. That is one Christian curse word that seems to hurt worse than any other kind of curse word! Why is that? Because no Christian wants to be rejected—by people or by God. We know Jesus gave His strongest condemnation to the Pharisees because they were religious (outwardly). When people call other Christians religious, it implies that they can't find any use for those people and that God rejects their labors before Him. That may or may not be true, but it sows doubt into the people called "religious," which often provokes them to violate their standards and even go to extremes of the flesh and soul in order to prove the "religious" title false.

This is sad and many people have shipwrecked their lives in the spirit because of this attack. And that is what it is—*an **attack** from the devil.* There *is* a difference between disciplining our bodies and souls and doing things based on religious duty. People often can't see the difference, especially if others are more disciplined than they are. And yet, being religious *is* a dangerous counterfeit to living a disciplined spirit life.

TELLING THE DIFFERENCE

How can we avoid being religious? God spoke this to me one time, and I believe it will set a lot of people free: *"You will never be religious if, in all your discipline, you will truly love people."* Love makes the difference.

That is the whole point of First Corinthians 13. Jesus was extremely disciplined in His soul and body, was misunderstood at times, was never ruled by public opinion, and yet was never religious. He loved God, and He loved people. And no matter what else they accused Him of doing or being, they could never accuse Him of not loving people or not doing good to them.

Love is the key. Love will make the real difference in our spirit life training. Love has to be the bottom line in all our discipline of flesh and soul. This is because the things of the spirit have to be transferred into the lives of people to bless *them*, to build *them*, not merely to build *us* or make *us* look good before others.

Satan is the author of religion, but at one time he was the "most spiritual" in Heaven. What led to his fall? He looked to himself, putting his own image before others. Yes, he was spiritual, but he had no love and became full of pride. He has discipline; he built rank and order in his demonic kingdom. The only thing that makes our discipline any better than this cherub's is our foundation of selfless love for God and for others. The more spiritual we are, the more relatable we must become because the more love compels us to bless others. We tap deeper into the spirit because we know we must have more to give to the multitudes who need the tangible touch of God's love.

There is a song that says "More love, more power, more of You in my life." That is not a request; it is a declaration and progression of fact. Love demands power to express itself. Divine love and power lead to the expression of the Spirit of Jesus through our lives. So it is important to understand the distinction between being religious and living a disciplined spirit life.

NEEDING A STRONG SPIRIT

We already talked about some reasons to have a strong spirit, but let's go a bit further with Ephesians 3:16-19.

That He would grant you, according to the riches of His glory, to be strengthened with might through His Spirit in the inner man, that Christ may dwell in your hearts through faith; that you, being rooted and grounded in love, may be able to comprehend with all the saints what is the width, and length, and depth, and height—to know the love of Christ which passes knowledge; that you may be filled with all the fullness of God. (Ephesians 3:16-19).

We know that love is vital. We know that faith is vital. We know that to be filled with the fullness of God is our dream come true. But all of that comes *after* being strengthened with might in our spirits. If we lack this strength, our love will be lacking. Our faith will be lacking. So we won't be filled with the fullness of God! A weak spirit means weak-spirit desires and weak-spirit ability. We need to be strong in spirit to have faith to change the impossible. Otherwise, our minds' doubts will drown out our spirits immediately.

It takes a strong spirit to walk in love; otherwise, the moment someone makes a mistake or offends us, our emotions lash out in hurt and anger. Each of us needs a strong spirit to tell our flesh *no* and to keep our souls fed and stabilized with the fruits of the Holy Spirit. Only the strong spirit can obey the high call of God for our lives. Otherwise, we will be pulled around by the wind and waves of emotions, opinions, and popularity instead of the inner compass of the inner witness. A strong spirit can give a "knowing" of God's direction and Will in any situation.

NAVIGATING UNCHARTED WATERS OF THE FUTURE

In Heaven there is a constant downloading of revelation of God and truth. There is a light in God that reveals everything—past, present, future, spirit, natural, thoughts, potentials, and so forth. Our spirits are created from above—the realm of Heaven. They have the same light from God. The spirit becomes like a flashlight; whenever it is turned on, it discovers hidden things that need to be known at that time. *"The spirit of a man is the lamp of the Lord, searching all the inner depths of his heart"* (Prov. 20:27).

Your spirit, when it is strong, can lead you through the darkness of ignorance in this world. It knows the difference between right and wrong and also can discern what is good, better, and best for *your* specific call and destiny.

THE ENERGIZING OF THE WILL

Here's something exciting. In Romans chapter 7, Paul explains the futility of the Will wanting to do right, but not having the power to do so. If the goal of our Wills is to align with the Will of God, how can we possibly do it? I hinted at this when we talked about having an inner response to God's leadings. How does this happen? Look at this again:

> *Therefore, my beloved, as you have always obeyed, not as in my presence only, but now much more in my absence, work out your own salvation with fear and trembling; for it is God who **works in you** both to **will** and to **do** for His good pleasure* (Philippians 2:12-13).

The word *works* in verse 13 is key. The original Greek translation for this is the word *energeo*, from which we derive the word *energy*. This says that God will literally *energize* our Wills to be able to choose His Will! Look at Ephesians 3:20: *"Now to Him who is able to do exceedingly abundantly above all that we ask or think, according to the power that **works** in us...."*

"Works" is that word *energeo* again! God is able to do His Will in such a powerful way in our lives (even above what our natural minds independent of Him could put together), according to the power that *energizes* us! *How? From what?*

Step back to Ephesians 3:14-16:

> *For this reason I bow my knees* [that means he is praying] *to the Father of our Lord Jesus Christ, from whom the whole family in heaven and earth is named, that He would grant you, according to the riches of His glory, to be strengthened with might through His Spirit in the inner man.*

It is only through the strengthening by the Spirit of God and the feeding of the spirit part of us that we will have the *energy* to do the Will of God. This energizing will rise up inside us like a tidal wave, and suddenly it will seem easy to do the Will of God as our Wills surf on this wave of energy! We can make so many New Year's resolutions to stop smoking, lose weight, to be a better person—but we don't have the strength to carry them through. This is why it is so important that we pay attention to the exercises later in this section to see how to energize our spirits! It's a priority!

ABSORB, THEN DO

Let me give a foretaste of this in picture form: God is like the sun. When a flower senses the energy radiating from the sun, it turns toward the sun, and as it absorbs this energy, it grows and grows. We are like the flower. Opening up our lives to worship God is like the flower opening up to absorb the sun's energy. We can hear, "Do this; don't do that," but that's not really the problem. We *want* to obey; we just don't have the energy! We must just stop and love on Him first, and *then* our spirits will absorb the energy radiated back at us to position our bodies to surf into the Will of God! As it is written, *"...You shall worship the Lord your God, and Him only you shall serve"* (Luke 4:8b).

Notice the order here: It is only *after* you worship Him that you can be energized to serve Him. Feeding your spirit first will make doing the Will of God much simpler. For example, if you are a millionaire and you want to go eat at the best place, the choices are quite simple. Money is not an object; you're able to just go for the best, right? But if you are quite poor and want to eat at the best place, the choice is much harder because you don't have the power to do it!

In other words, the more power we have, the simpler it is to make the best choices—and with less effort. Really, the lack of power blinds us from seeing the best choices. This is why people struggle with the question, "What is the Will of God for my life?" Never mind for now. First we must go to Acts 1:8 and get filled with power in the spirit part of us. Then, as our spirits grow in energy, this question will *no longer* be a struggle.

HOW OUR SPIRITS CAN TRANSFORM OUR IMAGE

When our spirits are strong, they can override the weaknesses of our personalities. There are weaknesses that every personality has— things that frustrate, intimidate, and limit the potential that God has put inside us. But within our spirits, at the very time we need it, there rises a strength, a boldness, a peace, a joy, and a confidence that can break us through in times where we formerly would have failed. It's like a "new us" emerges that shakes off the past and our personalities are branded from the flash of our spirits as they imprint themselves afresh on our souls. *"Then the Spirit of the Lord will come upon you, and you will prophesy with them and be turned into another man"* (1 Sam. 10:6). The more this happens, the faster our souls will be transformed into the image of Christ.

FORCING OUR SPIRITS TO
RISE TO THE SURFACE

My experience with fellow missionaries who were sent out around the world showed me this in a very real way. I knew their different personalities from Bible school and how they typically behaved within the U.S. culture. But when they were taken into third world countries where they were forced to live out of the strength of their spirits, radical changes began to take place within them. Demands came upon them daily for the sick, lost, poor, and dying. In their souls and bodies, they did not have the resources to handle this!

They were forced to dig into the spirit part of them and do what they were trained to do—heal the sick, cast out devils, prophesy God's Word, and save the lost. Daily they were pushed beyond their limits, physically and mentally. They were forced to remind themselves of the passion of God for these people and had to acknowledge God's ability within them to meet the demand. So, in each case, their spirits were forced to the surface continually—healing the sick, preaching to multitudes, casting out devils, worshiping God in the jungle—because there was no one else to talk to really except the bugs and people who didn't understand their English humor very well! They had to truly laugh because of the joy of God in these situations; it became a raw *choice* instead of something stimulated by Hollywood.

SHAPED BY THE FLOWING IN THE ANOINTING

So after a year or two, when I next saw the missionaries, it was amazing to see the transformation. I could tell that the anointing had actually changed and shaped their personalities into something new, something more powerful. It became easier for them to pull up this ability from the spirit, and they were no longer dependent on getting "drunk" on the American culture for their satisfaction. This change forced their appetites to change gradually as well. They no longer seemed to fit very well with those who were driven by the flesh and the soul. But this "spirit-branding" upon their personalities was still attractive as they transitioned from being followers with knowledge to leaders with influence and experience.

I too experienced this, and the greatest change I noticed was in the way I felt and reacted to situations. This "flame" of God would rise up more often, and I knew it was the strength of my spirit reacting to situations. I could feel its hungers, desires, and abilities. It was in me all along, but had never been pulled on or demanded to rise up to the challenges of life. My soul had once learned how to cope, but now my spirit had learned how to rise!

RICH ON THE OUTSIDE; POOR ON THE INSIDE

I have seen some of the wealthiest people and some of the poorest. I have seen the powerful and the destitute. But the greatest treasure I have ever seen lives inside the house of our flesh and souls—it is the untapped potential of our spirit. We could be the wealthiest people alive, but without a developed spirit, there is a weakness, an emptiness, and a fear that is constantly within. It is the root of vulnerability and unpredictability about the future that causes even the most wealthy and powerful to hide. They know deep inside that they are just mere humans. They know that time and chance could change at any time for them. When tragedies happen, then it all comes out, and they turn out to be just like anyone else. Again, I come to the point that I started with in this training. The Israelites were given a Promised Land, but we have a promised *nature*. We must possess this life in the spirit. It is something that can never be taken from us.

EVERYONE WANTS TO BE A HERO

When the spirit within us is strong, we have the revelation that we can shout the truth: "Greater is He who is in me than he who is in the world!" (See 1 John 4:4.) Every movie about a hero tells about something inside that individual that gives them the ability to overcome obstacles. Everyone intuitively knows that they should have this and can have this. (Otherwise, Hollywood wouldn't have such a continual market for it!) Unfortunately, most of what Hollywood displays is fantasy. It never tells us the truth of what it takes to build a strong spirit and possess this life that God promised us. But the most important step of our training is next: the exercises necessary to build our spirits. With a strong spirit, being a real superhero comes *naturally* (in a manner of speaking).

ENDNOTE

1. Smith Wigglesworth, "Life in the Spirit," smithwigglesworth.com, http://www.smithwigglesworth.com/sermons/eif10.htm; accessed January 2, 2011.

"THE SPIRIT—THE REAL PERSON" REVIEW

1. Our _____ is who we really are.

2. Read Philippians 1:21-24. *When we put the spirit part of us first, two things happen.* Note them below and explain why this is so.

    1) _____

    2) _____

3. The spirit keeps getting stronger and stronger as it is _____ more and more (see 1 John 4:4).

4. Your spirit is the _____ that displays the _____ of the _____ of God.

5. Everything we need to be equipped for victory, health, wisdom, love, and prosperity is ours because _____ ____ _____.

6. Read Ephesians 3:16-19. Based on what Paul knew was within the believer, *what did he pray for the Ephesian believers first in this prayer?*

7. What is a priority in God's eyes?

8. Read Ephesians 1:3; 2:5b-6. We can change environments and other things to make them productive for God because of the authority given to us in our _____ as we put our _____ _____.

9. When someone's spirit is strong, there is no situation where that person needs to feel _____.

    Why is that? _____

10. A strong spirit will impact people's lives and hearts in deep and lasting ways because it can build something that

_____ the eternal and will leave its mark for a _____ and beyond.

11. Note and discuss some of the signs of a strong spirit, below:

_____

_____

_____

_____

12. Even though we have perfect spirits at salvation, Ephesians 3:16 indicates that our spirits *can* get even *stronger.* This is both a _____and a _____.

13. Our healthy relationship with God is built upon _____, which is done through our spirit.

14. List some of the ways God communicated with people in the Old Covenant. Why are these not so good for those of us under the New Covenant?

_____

_____

_____

_____

_____

15. Read John 16:7,12-13. What right did Jesus give the believer's spirit when He was raised from the dead?

16. What is the New Covenant privilege talked about in Hebrews 10:16?

17. God wants to communicate directly to us _____ _____ _____, not through our bodies or our souls.

18. Read First Corinthians 2:9-10,12. How does God reveal things to us?

19. As long as we are aligned with the Word, we can expect the things that God gives us to be both _____ and _____ to ourselves and others (see Luke 11:11-13).

20. According to Galatians 5:19-21 and Second Corinthians 7:1, we are to keep our spirits' connections _____ _____ on God and His purposes. *Why is this so important even to New Covenant believers?*

21. Jesus is our example of the most _____ person on Earth. Yet, while being this way, how did He relate to all kinds of other people on Earth? _____

    _____

22. Why don't Christians like to be accused of being "religious?"

23. Being religious is a counterfeit to living a _____ spirit life.

24. We will never be _____ if, in all our discipline, we will truly _____ people.

25. Both divine _____ and _____ lead to the expression of the Spirit of Jesus through our lives.

26. Love and faith are both vital, but they come _____ being strengthened with might in our spirits!

27. What are some other reasons we need to have a strong spirit?

_____

_____

_____

_____

_____

28. Read Proverbs 20:27. A strong spirit can lead you through _____ _____ because it knows right from wrong and (most importantly) what is_____ for *your* call or destiny.

29. In Philippians, 2:12-13 we learn that God will_____ our Will to be able to choose His Will.

30. It is through the strengthening and the feeding of our inner spirits that we have the _____ to do the Will of God. This is why the upcoming spirit exercises are so important!

31. Also, when your spirit is strong, it can _____ the weaknesses of your personality (see 1 Sam. 10:6). The more this happens, the faster your soul will be transformed into the image of Christ.

32. When people are pushed beyond their limits physically and mentally in ministry, the spirit part of them can be "forced" to the _____. This continual breakout flash of the spirit causes us to become "spirit-branded," which reshapes our personalities to no longer be driven by the _____ and the _____. The spirit learns how to rise up as an automatic reflex.

33. The greatest wealth any of us has is the _____ _____ of our spirits. Without a developed spirit,

there is always a deep inner _____, _____
and _____ that is just waiting to be exposed.

34. When the spirit within us is strong, we can shout confidently:
"_____ __ ___ _____ __ __ _____ _____ __
_____ __ __ _____ _____!"

35. In preparation for the next "Building a Strong Spirit" exercises,
write down some of the results that you have learned will manifest
from having a strong spirit. (See questions 11 and 27 for some examples, plus any other insights found in the reading so far.)

36. *Now, begin to imagine your life with these characteristics.*

_____

_____

_____

_____

_____

_____

_____

_____

_____

CHAPTER 11

BUILDING A STRONG SPIRIT

Building a strong spirit is all about giving it what it likes to feed on. There are things that the spirit part of us gravitates toward and hungers for. *What we feed grows stronger; what we starve gradually dies.* So what do our spirits hunger for?

1. THE WORD OF GOD

This is no surprise, but this is without a doubt number one. Jesus made a choice that He would rather starve His flesh than neglect the Word of God. *"But Jesus answered him, saying, 'It is written: "Man shall not live by bread alone, but by every word of God"'"* (Luke 4:4). The Word of God simply does something to the spirit within us; it imparts life, strength, and energy. It's difficult to explain *why* or *how* it does this; nevertheless, Peter says, *"as newborn babes, desire the pure milk of the word that you may grow thereby"* (1 Pet. 2:2). It gives our spirits life for growth.

Hear It

The Word can be ingested in many different ways. The first way is by *listening* to it. I say this is first because *"Faith comes by hearing, and hearing by the word of God"* (Rom. 10:17). The Bible talks so much about being careful *who* we hear, *what* we hear, and *how* we hear. *What* should be the Word of God. *Who* should be someone who can speak the Word with the integrity, spirit, and strength that God Himself would say it with. *How* we should hear is with an attitude that knows that these are the very words of the Creator of the universe. We listen with intensity and respond. We have so many ways to hear the Word of God—there is Bible on tape, CD, mp3, radio, television, and so forth! There was a season where I only would play the Bible on tape in my car when I would drive. I wore those tapes out, but it built me up so much.

We can also listen to good preaching. Good preaching can get the Word into us in a stronger way than we could just on your own. *We should be our own best preacher*, but God has set in the Church apostles, prophets, evangelists, pastors, and teachers to get the Word into our spirits with the gift God has given them.

Read It

Second, we must *read* it. This involves time without distractions. When we read it, there will be some words that will jump out of the page into our spirits. The Holy Spirit will emphasize certain words strongly that will cause our spirits to burn with intensity about that truth.

Write It

Third, we must *write* it. Why? Every king in the Bible was told to write for himself a copy of the law (see Deut. 17:18-20). He couldn't hire someone to do it for him; he couldn't photocopy or cut-and-paste it. There is something about taking the diligence to write for ourselves the Word of God. It gives us a sense of responsibility and intimacy with the Word that God requires. It is a way to *not* skip over any words in a verse, and it is also a tool for memorization.

Memorize It

Fourth, we must *memorize* it. We have talked about this already in the chapter on the memory part of the soul, but memorization is vital.

The previous three ways are nothing if they don't lead to this fourth step! Every failure in the Bible was through forgetfulness of the Word.

Meditate on It

Fifth, we must *meditate* on it. This involves two smaller steps: *contemplation* and *declaration*. Contemplation is thinking intently about the full meaning of what was heard or read. Our spirits love this. *"My heart was hot within me; while I was musing, the fire burned. Then I spoke with my tongue..."* (Ps. 39:3). Contemplation causes the spirit to ignite the meaning of the Scripture with the soul. Our memories recall the verse to our minds; our intellects begin to understand what each word really means; our imaginations begin to see its application; our emotions begin to come alive as we feel what God feels about its truth; and our Wills decide to take a course of action concerning it. The first response should be to *speak it out.* Declaring the Word begins to shape the spiritual world around us to conform to the manifestation of that Word.

> *"And he who has My Word, let him speak My Word faithfully. What is the chaff to the wheat?" says the Lord. "Is not My Word like a fire?" says the Lord, "And like a hammer that breaks the rock in pieces?"* (Jeremiah 23:28b-29)

This process of meditation is important. If we try to speak it before we contemplate it, the words will not have the effect desired, even though it is God's Word! God's Word is more than letters, syllables, and sentences. It is describing a *reality*. If our souls are not wrapped around the meaning of that reality (as much as we are able to), all that is coming out of our mouths is simply sounds and noises from our vocal cords. It must be powered by a faith from our hearts in the conscious reality of what those words mean. On the other hand, it is important to *speak* it, not just think it. God does not just think; He speaks and things happen. His power will not activate unless there is a revelation of His Will through Word and deed.

Surely the Lord God does nothing, unless He reveals His secret to His servants the prophets. A lion has roared! Who will not fear? The Lord has spoken! Who can but prophesy? (Amos 3:7-8)

And never forget the amazing promise of the power of believing and speaking in Mark 11:22-23:

So Jesus answered and said to them, "Have faith in God. For assuredly, I say to you, whoever says to this mountain, 'Be removed and be cast into the sea,' and does not doubt in his heart, but believes that those things he says will be done, he will have whatever he says."

What a word picture! So we must do the entire process of true meditation, which is contemplation and declaration, to be able to release the power of God's Word.

NECESSITY FOR SPIRITUAL LIFE

There is power in the Word of God. We were created in the image of God by the Word of God. We were born again by the Word of God. We are guided by the Word of God. It is described as light, water, food, air, fire (and much more)—the basic necessities of life. Without these we die. In the same way, if we don't feed our spirits with the Word, there is no way they can be strong. But more than that, it is *how* we put that Word into us that unlocks the full life-giving power of the Word to our spirits.

Why the Word Doesn't Work

The number one parable of Jesus was the parable of the sower (see Matt. 13:3-23; Mark 4:1-20). The seed represented the Word of God sent to four different kinds of hearts. If someone just carelessly throws out the seed (the Word of God), it will land on the surface of any of those kinds of hearts. In spirit life training, *we* are the sowers. We know that the problem is never the Word's lack of power. The problem is the sower's carelessness in planting the Word! It is a stupid farmer who does not plant with focus and intensity. Let's be honest. There are Bibles in so many forms and shapes all over the place. But strong spirits are precious few! *See, it is not just the power of the Word, but the power that pushes the Word that makes the difference.*

How It Goes in, How It Comes Out

How intensely do we hear the Word? If we listen to nice, story-telling preachers who are not intense—that Word will go in one ear, but out the other. How intensely do we read it? How focused are we to catch that key Scripture and write it down? How intense are we to memorize it? How intensely do we contemplate and boldly declare the Word? *Intensity in the sower will prepare the soil of the heart.* It will shatter the hard heart of unbelief and carelessness. It will drive the seed deep enough that it will be remembered in the time of trial. It will burn out the weeds of distractions and shape our habits to consistently apply that Word. *Then* it will produce results. It is only *how* the Word is sown that will unlock our spirits' life and power.

A Side Note to Preachers

Any preachers who do not focus on this technology of *how* to sow with intensity should either change or find another profession because they are sure to produce a deception in the hearers (see James 1:21-25). People think that if they hear and know the Word that automatically makes them doers. But if the Word is sown intensely enough, the soil will know what to do, the seed will know what to do, and the person will change and become a *doer*. Obedience to the Word shouldn't be a difficult thing. Mark 4:26-29 describes it as automatic, like seeds growing into ripe grain. Obedience *will* be automatic if the Word is sown with intensity! Preacher, intensely go through the five steps first; then the Word will come out of you as intensely as you put it in you.

2. WORSHIP

There is a buoyancy in the spirit part of us. I don't really know of another way to put it succinctly, but let me describe what I mean. When born-again people die, what do their spirits do? Do they just linger around, haunting people, floating over to family members with butterfly kisses for each one? I don't think so. Like balloons filled with helium, they shoot straight up to God in Heaven. It is like gravity reversed. If that is true, what is keeping our spirits down here right now? Our Earth suits. This is the weight that spirit has to deal with. But we cannot deny that, no matter how low we may feel, our spirits have a *continual* pull heavenward. Worship must embrace this fact and let our spirits soar to seek the face of God. *"With my soul I have desired You in the night. Yes, by my spirit within me I will seek You early"* (Isa. 26:9a).

Release Our Spirits

It is not hard for the spirit part of us to seek God; it is easy, even in the early morning, when our souls and bodies are not quite awake! If we are born again, *our spirits know the way to God's manifest presence.* All we have to do is release our hearts to Him in worship.

People have this idea that God is hard to find—not for our spirits! They can find Him easily. Our souls and flesh need the training to do this, but if we will relax and let our spirits lead the way, worship will be easy. People think they need the right music, the perfect song, the right leader. All that is nice and good. But what we *really* need is to release our spirits. Buoyancy means that we release our spirits to the higher things of God. Our spirits exalt God's attributes: His faithfulness! His love! His justice! His providence! His wisdom! His victory! His miracle-working power! His mercy! His favor! His beauty! His grace! His salvation!

Our spirits don't need a song to declare these things (even though they will use one easily). All our spirits need is a shout, a bold declaration, a heartfelt testimony. This is all a part of the true essence of worship.

Gazing Into a Mirror of Glory

Our spirits sees who they really are when they gaze into the face of God in worship. Our flesh and souls try to veil this truth, but worship strips those lies away.

> *Nevertheless when one turns to the Lord, the veil is taken away. Now the Lord is the Spirit: and where the Spirit of the Lord is, there is liberty. But we all, with unveiled face, beholding **as in a mirror** the glory of the Lord, are being transformed into the same image from glory to glory, just as by the Spirit of the Lord* (2 Corinthians 3:16-18).

We can start with praising *who* He is. We can use the attributes previously mentioned or use a psalm from the Bible or another truth that the Word declares about who He is. We can even simply boast about a testimony God did in the Bible (or modern times). Let's practice some of those things now!

Breathing in His Breath of Life

The next stage will lead to worship for who He is *to us*. This is done in a spirit of thankfulness, but it is deeper than that. It is coming face-to-face with the presence of the Lord, and it is not just a bold declaration. But it is an intimate "breathing-in" of who He is to you. It's not just, "You are awesome in Your ability to set people free!" But it becomes, "You are awesome in Your ability to set *me* free! You are awesome to *me* as *I see You* set people free!" There is a distinct difference as we transition to this level of releasing our spirits to grow stronger and burn brighter.

Impregnate, Saturate, and Detonate

Releasing our spirits to praise God impregnates and saturates the atmosphere to draw His presence to manifest. But transitioning to this level of worship causes our spirits to engage Him face-to-face. This level of worship is not necessarily quiet, nor does it have to be tender and pretty. Actually, it can be quite intense.

God is intense, and if we truly come face-to-face with Him, His fire will cause our spirits to boil with the same kind of intensity. The Bible talks about the angels, creatures, and elders who surround the throne of God, and they are intense beings who *cry* out to Him! That doesn't offend Him one bit. That lets Him know that *"...all that is within me* [will] *bless His holy name"* (Ps. 103:1).

As explained in the beginning, there is a buoyancy in the spirit of the believer. When worship is truly released, the spirit reaches a critical saturation point that causes all that is in us to rise. Our spirits are so energized that they launch our souls and bodies to the heavenly realms in worship. Arms are lifted, hearts are lifted, souls are lifted, heads are lifted, and voices are lifted. Everything in us explodes to meet Him! This intensity of worship can produce some amazing spiritual experiences.

3. PRAYING IN OUR NATIVE LANGUAGES

Our spirits love to pray. *"Watch and pray, lest you enter into temptation. The spirit indeed is willing, but the flesh is weak"* (Matt. 26:41). Jesus told us a truth about the battle between the flesh and spirit here. First, the flesh does not have the power to overcome temptation, and second, it does not enjoy praying at first. In this example, the disciples had the greatest preacher and example of prayer in front of them and *still* fell asleep while He was praying some of His most intense prayers. These disciples were handpicked by Jesus Himself, too. This tells us that even if we do have the best teacher, we still have to deal with our flesh. It cannot be ignored. It must be targeted, disciplined, and forced to comply with what our spirit within demands.

Our Spirits Love to Pray

Third, this verse tells us that our spirits are attracted to prayer! They love the realm of prayer and find strength in prayer. Ephesians 6:18 says that we are to be *"praying always with all prayer and supplication in the Spirit...."* No matter what kind of prayer we pray, the spirit part of our being is involved. What this should tell us is that our spirits are *not* the problem in prayer. Sometimes we think we have to (by the force of our Wills) "get into the mood" for prayer. Not true. Our spirits are ready to step into prayer at a moment's notice. We don't have to warm up with a nice song or background music. We can pray without "feeling in the mood" for it. Our souls may get into a habit of wanting these things, but our spirits don't need them to get a hold of God in prayer.

Prayer That Gets Results

James 5:16 says that the effective, fervent prayer of a righteous person is powerful. There are three ingredients to this: righteousness, effectiveness, and fervency. *Righteousness* is knowing our position before God as completely forgiven and holy because of Jesus' sacrifice and the transference of His righteousness to us. *Our physical and vocal posture must accurately represent this spiritual position.* We should stand boldly—heads up, smiles on our faces, with strong voices; we are sons and daughters of the Most High! We approach our Father and act like it before Him! "Oh no, that seems prideful," some may say. No, it's actually called *faith* in what God Himself has done and said about us. To do otherwise is something else called *disobedience.*

Next we need *effectiveness.* This is simply having an understanding of what the Word of God says about the subject we are praying about. This is important because He will not answer people based on their emotions alone, but based on whether they use the tool of prayer accurately to do His Will. God's Word is His Will. There is a time for the prayer of faith, the prayer of casting your cares on the Lord, the spiritual warfare prayer, intercession, thanksgiving, repentance, forgiveness, the prayer of agreement, and so forth. These (and more) are vital in their usage and timing. It would take another book to train in each one, but basically the point is knowing the Word of God accurately in prayer.

Last, the ingredient of *fervency* is needed. This is being passionate about what we are praying for. It is having the Word of God so strongly in our hearts that our emotions are stirred up in our determination to see it accomplished. It provides an extra bit of "push" to see our prayers answered. We know God's Word, and our emotions will not accept anything less than its fulfillment. *We may be surprised to know that this "little extra" is what makes the difference between prayers being answered, or not.*

4. PRAYING IN TONGUES

Praying in our native languages is important, but it is limited. It requires what our minds can grasp. There are worlds of understanding that the human mind cannot grasp or even handle at times. Praying in our native languages must involve our souls as a tool. They work hand-in-hand with our spirits. However, the born-again spirit is far more advanced than the soul, which must go through a process of renewal. God has given to people (who choose to receive it) the ability to bypass the limitations of their own natural minds and tap directly into the mind of God, praying that out. *"For he who speaks in a tongue does not speak to men but to God, for no one understands him; however in the spirit he speaks mysteries"* (1 Cor. 14:2). In Acts 2, when the Holy Spirit was poured out, each one received a deposit of the Spirit and began to speak in other tongues.

Opening the World of the Spirit

Ever since the tower of Babel, there have been differing languages in the earth to communicate with. In China there are Chinese dialects. In France there is French. In Poland there is Polish. In England there is English. In each of these countries, if we want things to be done, we must communicate in the native language. But what about in the "country" of Heaven? Praying in the Spirit, or speaking in tongues, opens up the world of the spirit to communicate and direct things there. When we pray in unknown tongues, we go directly to the source of things in the realm of the spirit, and deal with them there. We must understand that our weakness is that our minds do not know the source of the problem! There is a groaning in our spirits that suffers because of this tension between the mind and the spirit. This deep-seated need within ourselves to pray the perfect Will of God can only be met by this tool God has given us through the Holy Spirit.

> *Likewise the Spirit also helps in our weaknesses. For we do not know what we should pray for as we ought, but the Spirit Himself makes intercession for us with groanings which cannot be uttered. Now He who searches the hearts knows what the mind of the Spirit is, because He makes intercession for the saints according to the will of God. And we know that all things work together for good to those who love God, to those who are the called according to His purpose* (Romans 8:26-28).

Mental Bypass Straight to the Spirit

Basically, praying in the Spirit is a "hotline" straight to the Spirit of God and the Will of God. This is something I need to emphasize concerning spirit life training. Praying in the Spirit opens a crack between the natural realm and the supernatural realm. There are so many things of the spirit that can be learned and experienced merely because of the fact that praying in the Spirit is an activity that directly activates the

Holy Spirit without first having to have the soul in agreement at all. There are many things in spirit life training that are attempted through the process of trying to get the body and soul to line up with the spirit from the outside-in.

But inversely, praying in the Spirit works from the inside out. Our bodies directly will feel the sensations of what the Spirit is doing and feeling, and our souls are in a place of discovery, trying to catch what our spirits are doing. Our souls are more bystanders than required participants. The beauty of it is this: Our souls don't have to fully understand what is going on; our spirits are still doing an effective work through us.

Once we are practiced in it, this exercise can be shifted into a higher gear by putting our souls into agreement with what our spirits are doing on the inside. Every little sensation that God gives to our spirits, our souls magnify, causing our spirits to soar even more as our souls are no longer deadweight that our spirits have to drag along.

Journeying Into the Spirit

A practical exercise for this is simply setting aside time to *just* pray in the Spirit. Start with something like five or ten minutes. Later it can become easy to pray one, two, or three hours like this, and it will only seem like ten minutes passed. Our goal in this is—like in worship—to release our spirits. We first put our bodies into a place where they can stay awake and be free enough to participate. I personally like to walk and pray in the Spirit. It keeps my body in a non-distracting motion so it doesn't get sleepy. Sometimes I get into a rhythm of pacing back and forth, sometimes of walking in a circle (though not too tight or else I would get dizzy). Some people and in some places in the world, they kneel while swaying back and forth to keep their bodies awake and participating.

Either way, the point is to get our bodies active and then forget about them so we can concentrate in prayer. In our personal prayer times, this can be done anywhere that is not distracting to others. (This means that it is not recommended to practice this where there is much human traffic that can come through—the hallway, the living room, the lobby of your hotel, downtown sidewalks, the grocery store, and so forth.) The main reason for that is that they will probably try to distract us because they might not understand what we are doing! Especially considering what we are going to do next. Then we must simply open our mouths and pray in the Spirit, letting the words flow as freely as water, just like the promise in John 7:38-39a:

> "He who believes in Me, as the Scripture has said, out of his heart will flow rivers of living water." But this He spoke concerning the Spirit, whom those believing in Him would receive....

The more fearful we are of our surroundings or the more doubtful we are of what God is saying through us, the more that river of words will squeeze up to become a trickle. We must give our voices strength and boldness, releasing and feeling the force of what the Spirit of God is speaking through us. Volume is extremely helpful because it provides an expression of freedom to our spirits. It blasts through the resistance and intimidation we feel coming against us. (At the very least, we should have enough volume for our own ears to hear what we are saying, but not a lot of breakthroughs will come from just that level alone.)

New vocal expressions, words, or languages will begin to bubble up; don't be afraid. We must relax and let them openly flow—stronger, freer, and bolder. Our bodies may start to have urges to move—lifting up the hands, waving them in the air, shaking and trembling, or other motions. Our feet may feel like marching, dancing, or jumping—this is not wrong. This is because our spirits are moving our bodies to participate with them, giving passion to the prayer! What is wrong is if we feel something is trying to choke us or plug up our praying in the Spirit. That is simply the attempt of the devil to stop us from praying. The solution is to take a deep breath and keep praying, persistently, with more authority, and louder, if possible.

Eventually a sense of freedom and release will come, we will no longer feel that pressure on our vocal expressions, and we can keep praying freely. We may not have known what just happened, but we just won a victory in the realm of the spirit. We must not stop praying at that point, but press on a bit further to see what else God has for us after that. When we pray in the spirit, our goal is not merely freedom for our spirits, but taking more ground in the spirit. When we feel that it is time to stop for right then, we must always thank God for what He has released to us during that time. We can tell our spirits that the next time we go into prayer we will start right at the point we left off at in our previous prayer time. Believe it or not, we can do this. We will waste less time and can go further with God.

Interpret for Edification

The Bible speaks of the amazing ability of praying in the Spirit to edify our minds through interpretation back to ourselves. Our spirits already are built up and edified through simply praying in the Spirit (see 1 Cor. 14:4), but there is a way our minds can also be greatly blessed by this release of the river of God.

> *Therefore let him who speaks in a tongue pray that he may interpret. For if I pray in a tongue, my spirit prays, but my understanding is unfruitful. What is the conclusion then? I will pray with the spirit, and I will also pray with the understanding. I will sing with the spirit, and I will also sing with the under-standing* (1 Corinthians 14:13-15).

So what is the process by which this edification happens? We first simply begin to pray in the Spirit, keeping our minds focused on God. It is very important not to let our minds wander! We keep praying and, in a sense, "listening" on the inside. While we do this, we inwardly ask and seek God for what He is saying through us. At first it may seem like we get a word or two here and there, kind of like tuning a radio and catching the sound of a couple stations as we pass by. Don't worry, just keep asking and seeking God. Often after we ask God for this interpretation (we do have to ask), we come to a place where we are satisfied or "full" after praying in the Spirit for a while. At that point, we can stop speaking in tongues and wait upon God for what He will say, keeping a "listening ear" open to Him.

What will bubble up into our minds could be a couple of words or a phrase; we should just begin to speak it out, no matter how strange it sounds. Instead of being afraid, we should speak the words with the same vocal cadence and intonation that they come to us in; this will help the flow of the words. We should keep speaking them out until the flow just seems to stop, without trying to ponder those words and make something up with our minds that would seem to fit with what we just said (we will know on the inside that it doesn't really fit). Instead, we just take what flows forth for what it is. It is good to write it down. It may not make sense right away; but we are just practicing right now. In time it will become easier and more accurate. These words could be praise, exhortation, counsel, direction, comfort, correction, or sometimes prediction. We end by thanking God for what He has told us and let Him confirm everything with the Word. As we use these words in prayer, we'll see what else God gives us to expand our understanding of how to apply these things to our lives.

Encouraging Ourselves in the Lord

I can't emphasize strongly enough how encouraging these times are. Everyone feels lonely and discouraged at times. We don't always have people around us to build us up and give us the exact words of encouragement that we need. Sometimes we feel like failures and like everyone's against us. But the Holy Spirit is on the inside, and He will give us the precise inspiration that we need. It is so amazing! It literally *breathes life* into us.

Every time He has spoken to me like this, those words have fed and blessed me for many years afterward. That is the nature of His speech; His words have eternal life in them. They energize us and spur us on to our highest destinies. We may come into our place of prayer so depressed, but after priming the pump of the gift of the Holy Spirit—praying in the Spirit, interpreting, praying in the Spirit, interpreting again—we will be flying on cloud nine! Those of us who have never prayed in the Holy Spirit or sought Him for the interpretation don't know the blessing they are missing—or maybe *needing*. Let's seek and receive it today!

5. OBEDIENCE

We saw in Luke 4:4 how Jesus quotes that Scripture passage that says that people do not live by bread alone, but by every Word that proceeds from the mouth of God. This is talking about our spirits' hunger for the Word of God, but the actual context Jesus used this in was combating a temptation. The temptation was to try to get Jesus to turn stones into bread. This temptation (as in every temptation) was to get Jesus to obey the devil's command to fulfill His fleshly desire. That is why Jesus responded that He received nourishment from the Word of God, but specifically through *obeying* the Word of God!

Crisis of Choice: A Chance to Feed Your Spirit

Our spirits receive strength from obeying the commands of God. In this process of temptation, a choice must be made: *Who will be obeyed? God or the devil?*

God will always point to feeding the spirit first. *"But seek first the kingdom of God and His righteousness, and all these things shall be added to you"* (Matt. 6:33). The devil will point to feeding our flesh and souls first! Whoever we obey, one part of us will be fed, while the other part will suffer. When we obey the devil through feeding our flesh and souls first, our spirits will suffer. When we do this, we can feel the effect on the inside. We really feel something quenched deep inside. Something seems to die. That is the life of our spirits being choked. It is true, when we obey God, our flesh and souls *will* suffer momentarily (see Rom. 8:5-13). However, we can feel the difference in what happens on the inside of us! Something seems to come alive. Energy begins to pulsate through us from our spirits. Sometimes obedience may seem embarrassing to our minds or flesh, but inside there comes a joy and freedom that our carnal minds can't quite explain.

Hidden Sources of Energy

Our spirits *love* to obey God. Whenever the spirit can get the body and soul in line to obey, the Spirit of God imparts something fresh to nourish our spirit. True, our physical bodies do need food, but Jesus referred to a deeper hunger to obey God.

> But He said to them, "I have food to eat of which you do not know." Therefore the disciples said to one another, "Has anyone brought Him anything to eat?" Jesus said to them, "My food is to do the will of Him who sent Me, and to finish His work" (John 4:32-34).

To the natural mind, this is a strange metaphorical saying. But Jesus was not talking about a metaphorical saying; He was talking about a spiritual reality. For example, we could be physically hungry, but we really sense God wants us to tell someone a word from Him. It could be witnessing or a gift of the Spirit. Afterward, we feel what happened to us on the inside. True, our physical bodies could be still hungry, but some kind of energy came into us. It's not just adrenaline from the situation, but it is a life-giving energy. This is true for a lot of situations where our flesh and souls come into direct conflict with our spirits. It could be speaking the truth, obedience in tithing and giving, loving difficult people, serving God when it's not easy, choosing to pray and believe when we hear bad news, and so forth. Our flesh hates it so much at first, but our spirits feel so good, so strong!

I have been in places where, before I would preach, I felt physically sick. My flesh would say, "This is too hard. I am going to either faint or throw up." My mind would say, "Yes, and that would not be a good testimony of the Gospel's power! It's wisdom to postpone this and wait until I feel well." But my spirit would tell me of the need of these people to hear the Word; my spirit would remind me that God has sent me to preach good news no matter how I feel. So I would decide to step out in faith, and soon after I would start preaching, the energy of God would come into me and from my head to my toe I would feel great. What happened? As soon as I stepped out in obedience, my spirit received the nourishment it needed to overthrow the work of the enemy.

Temptation: Stepping Stone to Greater Power?

The greater the challenge to obedience, the greater the strength is that comes from that obedience. For this reason, it seems that every temptation of the devil can be used to make our spirits stronger *if* we continually make the choice to obey God every time. Jesus was baptized in the Spirit before His temptations, but it was only after He obeyed God during His time of temptation that a new power came into Him. *"Then Jesus returned in the power of the Spirit to Galilee, and news of Him went out through all the surrounding region"* (Luke 4:14).

People have wondered about Paul's thorn in the flesh—was it sickness? We don't have evidence for that, but Paul does say that it was a messenger of satan. He wanted it gone, but God showed him what He was giving Paul instead.

Concerning this thing I pleaded with the Lord three times that it might depart from me. And He said to me, "My grace is suffi-cient for you, for My strength is made perfect in weakness." Therefore most gladly I will rather boast in my infirmities, that the power of Christ may rest upon me. Therefore I take plea-sure in infirmities, in reproaches, in needs, in persecutions, in distresses, for Christ's sake. For when I am weak, then I am strong (2 Corinthians 12:8-10).

Now this passage seems to be contradictory, except in light of the understanding of spirit life. Paul was saying that when his flesh and soul were tempted and tormented by satan, when he made the choice to obey God, *a new grace, a new power, came into his spirit,* which made him overcome these obstacles. The greater the obstacle, the greater the power. This is where we don't like it however: it is only when the chal-lenge comes and the choice to obey is made, that the power comes into our spirits! We want the equipping before the challenge, but this type of spirit nourishment only comes cooked in the heat of opposition.

Shift Into High Gear; Run the Devil Over

God doesn't lead us into temptation, but the devil does try to get in our way. We can complain if we want to, but God isn't worried. If we will simply determine to obey, God will give us the power to run the devil over in front of everyone. This was the whole point of the ten plagues of Egypt. The devil resisted God's people to keep them from obeying Him again and again while Moses determined to obey God again and again.

Then the Lord said to Moses, "Rise early in the morning and stand before Pharaoh, and say to him, 'Thus says the Lord God of the Hebrews; "Let My people go, that they may serve Me, for at this time I will send all My plagues to your very heart, and *on your servants, and on your people, that you may know that there is none like Me in all the earth. Now if I had stretched out My Hand and struck you and your people with pestilence, then you would have been cut off from the earth. **But indeed for this purpose I have raised you up, that I may show My power in you, and that My Name may be declared in all the earth"""*** (Exodus 9:13-16).

God gets glory (and pleasure) from giving His people power to run over and humiliate the devil as they obey Him. God meant this to be a lesson to His people that even though challenges might come, if we still obey, God's power will provide for us. Very few people understood this. Even the Book of Job teaches the same lesson. We must understand that to activate and build powerful spirits, we have to obey God during opposition. If we choose to back down, our spirit also backs down into a corner. If we choose to rise up, God puts power into our spirit to press through and break the devil's back.

6. FIGHTING THE DEVIL

This may seem like the last exercise, but it has a crucial difference. The previous exercise's focus was on obeying God. This has to be the first focus. We don't chase the devil all the time because that just leads us out of the Will of God. Jesus chose to do the will of God as number one, and when the devil got in the way, He destroyed his works. However, this fact is true: When we fight the devil, our spirits get stronger instead of weaker. Ephesians 6:10-17 gives the clear reality that we *do* fight with demonic forces. What do we fight them with? Yes, the armor listed in Ephesians 6. But where does that armor go? On our bodies? No, it goes on our spirits! It is interesting and important that the spirit is related to a *sword*. What is a sword used for? A discussion?

No, it is used for a fight. The spirit within each of us is meant to fight. *It gets stronger and sharper in the fight.* As long as we keep swinging that sword, we get stronger. When we let it down, we get weaker and weaker. If we keep our spirits in an offensive, aggressive posture toward the devil, we will see our spirits' strength increase.

Spiritual Reaction Against Evil

Every time the spirit of a believer reacts against evil, unbelief, corruption, fear, or any of the things written in Galatians 5:19-21 *("... adultery, fornication, uncleanness, lewdness, idolatry, sorcery, hatred, contentions, jealousies, outbursts of wrath, selfish ambitions, dissensions, heresies, envy, murders, drunkenness, revelries, and the like...")*, the spirit gets sharper and stronger. We can feel it. So, what kind of reaction should we have? Well, each of these evils in Galatians 5 is a desire of the devil's Will, and when we use our Wills to say to these things, *"No!* I will not do that; it is *wrong,"*—that is a reaction.

Another reaction would be to say *yes* to the opposite right thing. For instance, take the top thing on the list: "No! I will not commit adultery! I choose to love my wife! The Word says 'I am dead to sin and alive to God in Jesus Christ' and 'husbands love your wives as Christ loved the Church and gave His life for it!'" Or we could exercise both a negative and positive reaction by saying, "No! Adultery is wrong! Yes! I will keep my body pure for Him! The Word says, I am bought with a price, and I am to glorify God in my body and spirit!"

Either way, we feel the reaction in our spirits. We *react* against lies! We *react* against fear! We *react* against ungodliness! And we also react *for* the positive things of God! These reactions will help greatly in sharpening our spirits.

Don't Be Distracted By a Counter Reaction

When we react, the devil reacts back. Then we have to swing that sword accurately. Antagonistic thoughts will hit our minds. People will *not* just stand by and be quiet when we react; they will get mad, challenge us, and try to knock the sword of the Word and Spirit out of our hands. ("Who do you think you are? You don't know what you are talking about! You don't have a right to challenge this! You are arrogant!")

David's brother reacted to how David reacted to Goliath (see 1 Sam. 17:28). The same thing will happen to us. The temptation is then to get angry at the people, but that is the devil's distraction. At all times we must keep a strong *love* for people. It is not a battle about our personal opinions, but over God's *truth*. *"Is there not a cause?"* (1 Sam. 17:29). A new strength will come into us as we react strongly to what we see, feel, or think based on the Word of God.

Being "Casual" Won't Advance the Cause

If we feel the devil resisting something good, something supported by the Word of God, we must not just be bystanders and watch. We get *no* new strength that way! We must get behind the cause and say "Yes, that's right! The Word says...!" We must use our swords and swing them to further that cause! The only thing the devil has to bow to is a greater force against him, so we need to be determined to fight until we win. The more we swing that sword against the devil and resistance, the stronger and sharper our spirits will get. The fact is, we cannot control everything that happens to us in the world. The devil will purposely throw something in front of our eyes, ears, or thoughts in order to tempt us. That can be OK *if we react against it!* Reacting strongly and fighting against temptation trains us for battle. If we do not react, we will lose the battle and have to go back to God for mercy and cleansing, and we will have to rebuild our spirits' strength again.

The attitude that leads us to not react is what I call *"being casual."* Being casual means that we aren't alert at all times. We treat these ungodly things lightly, as if they are a joke: "Oh, it's no big deal. I know these things can't affect me in Christ." It can also be defined as taking things as they come. The devil and his work floats by us and, as long as he isn't affecting our personal space, we just leave him alone. We think, *As long as I leave him alone, he will leave me alone.* But this is not true. He only comes to steal, kill, and destroy (see John 10:10). He is just seeing how close he can get to us unnoticed so he can damage those close to us and eventually ruin our lives as well.

So he lets tales of cancer float by us, jokes about drunkenness and sex float by us, news about bribery and corruption float by us, co-workers who complain and gossip float by us, and if we don't develop resistance in those situations, when he finally unloads on us directly, it will be too late for us to get aggressive. As they say, "The best defense is a good offense." When we are always prepared to attack, the devil will think twice before trying to mess with us. The facts are: He is *not* God and does *not* have unlimited resources! If we are going to waste too much of his time and energy and if he knows that he will get little results for his efforts, he would rather spend time on easier targets.

I am not saying that we should jump out and attack people with our words, but instead have great compassion for them. We shouldn't purposely seek to start arguments; that's not what Jesus did. His thoughts of purity created a presence that led people to Him. When confronted, He used His words like a surgeon uses a scalpel, preserving people's value before God, yet striking at the root of the corruption in their lives or society. Inwardly, we have to have a fury against evil, but at the same time have great compassion for the people evil is hurting. We speak the truth in love because we are fighting to save people's lives.

It's Foolish to Tempt the Devil

People wonder why God wants us to be trained for war. Let's look at this passage:

Now these are the nations which the Lord left, that He might test Israel by them, that is, all who had not known any of the wars in Canaan (this was only so that the generations of the children of Israel might be taught to know war, at least those who had not formerly known it)... (Judges 3:1-2).

This fighting spirit strengthens our love for God even more. *"You who love the Lord, hate evil!"* (Ps. 97:10a). Some people try to act over-confident and put themselves into the battle by walking right into temptation, daring the devil to tempt them. They will purposely do things that they know will tempt them. They know they are tempted by alcohol, but walk into bars "to say hi." They know that they have a tendency to blow up in anger, but they want to just "give them a piece of advice." They know that pornography has trapped them and others before, but they just want to "look for a minute." Those kinds of people are foolish. This may seem contradictory, but sometimes the strongest reaction of our spirits is not to get involved. We can boldly get up *and walk out.* We can throw that DVD away (if it is our possession), turn off that radio station, tear up that magazine (if it is our possession), shut down that computer, and so forth. We must use our swords to cut those situations out of our lives.

Build a Wall and Fight the Devil, Too

Fleeing temptation is not weakness or fear; it is a bold reaction against it. As we walk away, we will feel that security and strength come into our spirits. We have just acted like Nehemiah, who fought the devil with one hand, but built a wall against fighting unnecessary battles with the other hand (see Neh. 4:14-17). The devil does not want any walls built. As mentioned before, our chief purpose is not to be fighting all the devils of the world, but to do the will of God. We must fight hard and furiously when the temptation pops up, but we shouldn't keep our walls down so we have to get involved with fighting every temptation that we choose to walk into! Paul said, *"All things are lawful for me, but all things are not helpful. All things are lawful for me, but I will not be brought under the power of any"* (1 Cor. 6:12). We are not afraid of any devil at all, but we will not be provoked out of the Will of God. Our spirits love a good fight (the only good fight is the one we win), but our spirits love the Will of God even more.

Building Our Spirits in the Proper Order

This is the *last* key to building a strong spirit. There are five keys that go before this one. Paul said, *"Finally"* be strong and fight the devil (see Eph. 6:10-17) after five other chapters of instruction! The *"finally"* is very important, however; without it, we can lose the ground we have gained in the first five exercises. And we can even learn to take ground if we learn to swing our swords effectively. Someone has said that 90 percent of our warfare is personal—disciplining our flesh and souls to get in line with our spirits in order to put it first and obey God. The stronger we can say *no* to our flesh and souls, the more the devil will feel it when we say *no* to him! If we win these internal battles first, we will be prepared soldiers for all other spiritual combat.

"BUILDING A STRONG SPIRIT" REVIEW

1. What we _____ grows stronger; what we _____ gradually dies.

2. The *first way to build our spirits* is the _____ of God (see Luke 4:4; 1 Pet. 2:2). It gives the spirit within each of us an almost unexplainable impartation of energy, strength, and life.

3. (a) The first way we ingest the Word is by _____ (see Rom. 10:17). Yet, we must be aware of the attitude with which we _____; we must _____ with _____ and _____. *Why is this important?*

   (b) Explain what is meant by being careful *"what* we hear, *who* we hear, and *how* we hear." *Why is this important?*

4. The second way to ingest the Word is to _____ it. The third way is to _____ it. Then we need to _____ and _____ on it.

5. (a) The entire process of meditation is _____ and _____ to be able to release the power of God's Word. God's Word is more than _____, _____, and _____. It is describing a _____!

   (b) How can one make this transition from speaking meaningless words to releasing the power of God's Word with our mouths?

6. Read Matthew 13:2-23 and Mark 4:1-20. It is not just the power of the Word, but the power that _____ the Word that makes the difference! We need to listen with _____.

7. If the Word is sown intensely enough, the hearer of the Word will become a _____ of the Word.

PRACTICAL TRAINING

Hold out your hand and, starting with the pinky finger and moving toward the thumb, name the five ways to ingest the Word:

1) Hear

2) Read

3) Write

4) Memorize

5) Meditate.

Why should they move in that direction? Because your grip is strongest, with your forefinger and thumb engaged, demonstrating that your grasp of the power of the Word is strongest when you get to the level of memorization and especially meditation.

Choose a good Bible-reading program. Approximately four to five chapters a day will get you through the whole Bible in a year and the New Testament twice. Read through the Bible out loud (using the Bible on tape, CD, or mp3 is good to speak aloud with also), stopping to write down Scriptures that jump out at you as you read with intensity. These are Scriptures you can put in your topical notebook (remember the memory exercises?) for memorization and meditation later.

Plan ahead because, in my experience, this will take approximately one hour each day.

Memorize those verses until they can arise instantly, and meditate on them thoroughly, to the point that the moment when you think of any one of them, energy floods your spirit and mind along those lines.

> *Don't stop even there, because as long as you keep squeezing those Scriptures, the juice keeps flowing!*

8. The second way to build our spirits is to _____. Our spirits have a _____ _____ toward Heaven.

9. Our spirits know the _____ to God's manifest presence!

    Discuss the ways of releasing your spirit in praise and worship. (*Look out; you might actually start to do it right now!*)

    Read Second Corinthians 3:16-18. What does it tell us that we gaze into when we look at the face of God in worship? Who else do we see when we worship? How important should that be to us?

10. This next step of worship is deeper as we transition past seeing who He is, to who He is ____ _____ in a very real and personal way.

11. When *"...all that is within* [us will] *bless His holy name"* we release our spirits to _____ and _____ the atmosphere with His presence, some amazing things happen.

PRACTICAL TRAINING

Speed praise! In this unique exercise, your goal is to see how fast you can release your spirit straight into high praise and then into the place where you "get lost" in worship—where you know you are face-to-face with Him in adoration with a strong sense of His presence rushing into the place. Can you manifest this in ten minutes? Five minutes? *One minute?* In that place, you can spend hours, but how long does it take you to get there to begin with? Also, how "strong" can you get it to become?

First, you may "piggy back" with a good praise and worship session from a CD or mp3. But you must be alone where you can move your body and voice without any sense of self-consciousness. Let the music be the support, but you must be free to fully participate with the song and the music, staying focused just as strongly as (or more strongly than) the people on the recording.

Second, you must build your *own* spiritual muscles once you have tasted that you *can* sense a strong tangible presence of God when you release your spirit in worship. This time, keep the music off and just use your raw Will to focus your own memory, imagination, and emotions on the attributes of God. You can sing your own songs, shout, declare, or release in a poetic cadence the psalms of the Lord from your spirit. Feel the ebb and flow of how these words are flowing from you and how one song or declaration jumpstarts another. This flow should transition into this "getting lost" in worship, not just sensing who He is, *but who He is **to you** here, now, and forever!* How strong this gets depends on how much of yourself you release to participate with Him! *Practice to see how fast you can get to this place in a very real way!*

12. The *third way to build strong spirits* is to _____ in our _____ _____. When we pray our spirits are involved. James 5:16 says that the effective fervent prayer of a righteous person gets results.

    How do we become righteous and behave as righteous people when we pray?

13. Effectiveness takes knowing the _____ of God _____ in prayer. Being passionate about what we are praying about and having our hearts and emotions stirred up is called _____. *This often makes the difference between prayers being _____, or not!*

PRACTICAL TRAINING

Put together the three ingredients of what it takes to pray a prayer that gets your spirit involved and brings results. Take it step by step and check yourself to see if you are actively including each ingredient.

Note your three prayer topics below:

1) _____

2) _____

3) _____

Now note the difference you feel on the inside, and don't forget to record the results of the prayer later.

14. _____ ____ _____ is the fourth way to build our spirits. It bypasses the natural mind and goes directly to the mind of God. Our minds don't know the source of the problem so we need to pray in the _____ of the spirit and deal with things there (see Rom. 8:26-28).

15. Praying in the Spirit opens a crack between the _____ realm and the _____ realm.

Discuss and describe what is happening to the rest of your soul and body when you are praying in the Spirit.

_____

_____

_____

Why is this exercise so unique from other aspects of spirit life training?

_____

_____

_____

16. Our goal in setting aside time to just worship in the Spirit by praying in tongues is to _____ our spirits. The ultimate reason we pray in the Spirit like this is to take more _____ in the spirit.

    What are some practical ways to exercise this on a regular basis?

    _____

    _____

    _____

    *What is **your** plan?*

    _____

    _____

    _____

    What are some things we have to be aware of and careful about when we are praying in the Spirit? What do we do in these situations?

    _____

    _____

    _____

17. First Corinthians 14:13-15 says we can ask God for an _____ of what we are praying in tongues. God is giving us an understanding of how to apply things to our lives.

    What is the process of how to practically do this?

    _____

    _____

18. God's words through the Holy Spirit in tongues and interpretation can _____ life into us. His words are containers of life and are an amazing blessing to us.

PRACTICAL TRAINING

Get a notebook that you will use solely for interpretation of your tongues (as well as prophecy) in your private prayer times. Record the days (dates), time spent in tongues, and any words that you have received. Use the exercises in this chapter and record your experiences as a result of this.

If you are doing this study with a group or a partner, share some of your experiences!

19. The fifth way to grow our spirits is through _____ the Word of God (see Luke 4:4).

20. Our spirits receive _____ from obeying the commands of God. The devil will try to have us feed our flesh and souls first. The flesh and soul may suffer a little at first, but when we are obedient, there is a joy and _____ that our carnal minds can't explain (see Matt. 6:33; Rom. 8:5-13).

21. Our spirits _____ to obey God, and obedience gives us spiritual energy (see John 4:32-34). Our spirits can receive the nourishment they need to overthrow the work of the enemy!

22. Every _____ of the devil can be used to make our spirits stronger ____ we continually choose to obey God every time; the greater the obstacle is, the greater the _____ is.

23. God gets _____ from giving His people power to run over the devil as they obey Him.

PRACTICAL TRAINING

Record five specific instances in which you made a conscious choice to obey God when it was difficult to do so. Note the results that you sensed in your spirit when the action was carried out.

ACTION	RESULT
1) _____	_____
2) _____	_____
3) _____	_____
4) _____	_____
5) _____	_____

---

24. Fighting _____ _____ is *the sixth way to grow a strong spirit.* Our first _____ is on obeying God, but we have to fight the evil one as well (see Eph. 6:10-17).

25. The Spirit is referred to working as a _____. A _____ is used for a fight!

26. The devil bows to a greater force. We must be _____ to fight until we _____.

27. Every time your spirit _____ against evil, your spirit gets sharper and stronger.

    What is the common response of other people in agreement with this evil when we do this?

    What is the proper response we should have toward people at all times?

28. The battle is not about anyone's personal _____, but over God's_____.

29. Don't be _____ by just being a _____ and _____. _____ the cause!

    Why is this statement important?

    What are some practical examples of this in everyday life?

    1) _____

    2) _____

    3) _____

30. We speak the _____ in _____ because we are fighting to save people's lives.

    How can we do the above examples and still act in great compassion?

31. Sometimes the _____ _____ of our spirits is not to get involved with things that are ungodly. We must boldly get up and _____ _____, cutting out bad situations in our lives.

32. Read First Corinthians 6:12. We are not to be _____ out of the Will of God.

33. Ninety percent of all our warfare is _____, disciplining our flesh and soul to get them in line with our spirits. The stronger we can say *no* to our flesh and souls, the more the devil will feel it when we say *no* to him.

PRACTICAL TRAINING

Pick a fight! Re-examine questions 27-29, and page 190. Think of three new areas about which you are presently "casual" or not forceful and make a conscious choice as to what you will and will not tolerate in the future.

WHAT ARE YOU *AGAINST?*	**WHAT ARE YOU** *FOR?*

1) _____ _____

2) _____ _____

3) _____ _____

Recognize three specific instances/circumstances in which you are "starting a fight" and have an opportunity to react in a practical way (even in your thought life), either *against or for* the instance/circumstance.

1)
    a. _____

    b. _____

    c. _____

2)
    a. _____

    b. _____

    c. _____

3)
    a. _____

    b. _____

    c. _____

CHAPTER 12

DEALING WITH RESISTANCE

At this point in our training, it is important to understand what is happening when we face problems during the training. People make the wrong kinds of excuses regarding the resistance they are facing. They don't know what is happening on the inside of them when they are being pushed to the point of breakthrough for their spirits. It is like when a plane is accelerating to the point of breaking the sound barrier. The plane starts shaking; it feels like it is about to fall apart! But that is not what is happening. It means that the plane is approaching the speed of sound and the pressure is building to the point of producing an explosion of sound called a *sonic boom*. The vehicle isn't the problem; it is just approaching a speed where it is shaking up some things.

UPSET, BUT DON'T KNOW WHY?

Normally, training works best when there is a *trainer*. Athletes, people at a new job, and so forth, normally cannot push themselves to the level of excellence required. Often they will do as much as they think they need to do and stop there. A trainer will push them beyond those self-imposed limits to help them discover a new level of performance within them. People normally realize this and will hire trainers for that purpose. When I would take people through some of these exercises, some had negative reactions. Some would get mad at me, and they didn't really know why! They felt uncomfortable as they approached these barriers in themselves.

The barriers could be in a lot of things, but the number one barrier is being unable to take direction! If someone has so much pride that merely listening to and obeying someone else's instructions is hard, it is going to be a long process! But if they can get past that, other barriers can rise up while training the emotions; dealing with memories; using the imagination; accepting what their intelligence doesn't understand yet; making their flesh obey them when it is distracted, tired, or hungry; forcing their Wills to take control of their beings; praising God with all their energy; praying in the Spirit loudly with all their heart and vocal expression; saying *no* forcefully to the devil and saying *yes* freely to God—and much more.

People would draw back and say, "I just can't do that!" I would ask why, and they would say something like, "It doesn't feel right," "It's uncomfortable," "It upsets me," and so forth. As a trainer, I listened, but I knew the end goal was in sight, so at that moment I didn't care how they felt in their emotions and flesh. I knew they would feel much better after they broke through the resistance. I also knew that what they were feeling was the barrier of the prison that their flesh and souls had put their spirits in.

TRANSFORMATION CAN BE PAINFUL AT FIRST

I know it *will* be painful for us to break out of what is familiar to us, but once our spirits are released, we will discover that our personalities have changed and we are happier and freer because of it. *Again, we don't know who we are. No one knows. We think we know, but it is only the Holy Spirit who made us who really knows. It is only through discovering our lives in the Spirit that we really bloom and discover what our potential is.*

So I put up with people's whining and suffering and kept pushing them until they fully participated with these exercises. I knew that their anger or frustration with me was only because they seemed to see me as the root of their discomfort. I knew that the real problem was in their flesh and souls. What I told them was this: "When you feel this frustration, it is the fire of God bringing up the junk in your flesh and soul. Great! Now what are you going to do about it? Hate the process? No, that won't solve anything. What needs to happen is that you keep pushing through the exercises and see that the feelings themselves are what need to be crushed. Those feelings are the voices of rebellion in your flesh and soul against God and your spirit. They are being directly challenged—perhaps for the first time in your life! It is actually a good thing that they are rising up so now they can be dealt with! Remember, your trainer is *not* the enemy."

What I was doing was reassuring them that because they were feeling this, *I knew we were on the right track.* If they didn't feel any resistance, that simply meant that they were choosing to dwell comfortably in this prison of the flesh and soul. *Everyone* has to deal with it, whether they are the pope, a pastor, an apostle, a homemaker, a businessman, an athlete, or a student.

RESISTANCE FORCES US TO RISE TO NEW LEVELS

More importantly, it is the resistance that is going to push us to the point of our miracles, the point of our breakthroughs, the point of releasing the strength in the spirit part of us. God had spoken to me about the story of blind Bartimaeus in the Bible—how *resistance was necessary for his miracle.* He was sitting by the road begging when Jesus passed him by. Bartimaeus didn't just passively think, *Oh, if God really wanted me to be healed, He would have had Jesus notice me sitting here.* (Stop and consider that fact for a moment!) Bartimaeus was going to make *sure* that he got His attention and that he would not quit until he got what he *knew* Jesus had for him. But even though Bartimaeus couldn't see to stop Him and didn't have anyone to help him, he knew how to use his voice. He raised his voice to cry out and grab Jesus' attention. His voice began to push its way through the crowd and the crowd didn't like it.

> Then many warned him to be quiet; but he cried out all the more, "Son of David, have mercy on me!" So Jesus stood still and commanded him to be called. Then they called the blind man, saying to him, "Be of good cheer. Rise, He is calling you" (Mark 10:48-49).

When we read this, we think how heartless these people were. If Bartimaeus had listened to them, he would have missed such a great miracle and stayed blind for the rest of his life. But what God spoke to me was this: "Would Bartimaeus have received his miracle if those people hadn't resisted him?" I thought about it, and actually it *was* because of their resistance, which caused him to *"cry out all the more"*! In the same way that the gale force winds of a storm cause the eagle to tilt its wings to soar to a higher altitude above the storm, so the force of their resistance caused Bartimaeus to reach deeper within himself to forcefully release a greater cry of faith. *Without the resistance, he wouldn't have gotten his miracle.*

When we know that what we demand is the Will of God, we learn to *enjoy* the resistance. It separates the serious from the slackers, the warriors from the wimps, and the determined from the daydreamers. It becomes a stepping-stone to build and release the strength necessary to break through to our miracles. Again, just as the eagle uses resistance to soar to greater heights, when we feel the resistance against the Word, against our praise, against our praying (both native language and tongues), against our obedience, or feeling the devil trying to push us to back off of him, we grit our teeth, double our efforts, and press in all the more! The resistance means we are entering a place of testing. God always has a great reward for us on the other side of passing that test! God is a rewarder of overcomers. *"He who overcomes shall inherit all things, and I will be his God and he shall be My son"* (Rev. 21:7).

We *must* face resistance head on. Until we stop hiding from what is uncomfortable, we cannot progress. People always are looking for shortcuts. This is probably why many people first picked up this book, thinking there would be a secret shortcut to spiritual development. Hopefully we have realized by now that hard work is still required, but now we have a workout strategy. As they say, "Plan your work, and work your plan!" But if you are *really* looking for a shortcut, here it is. Instead of trying to find the path of least resistance, *find the path of the **most** resistance in your training.* That is where you will find the greatest and quickest change. Whatever exercise is hardest and most boring for you to do, rejoice! You have found the point to overcome and manifest your divine sonship. When we learn to relish resistance, our spirits can really accelerate in their development and manifestation through us.

RECOGNIZE THE TREASURE IN DISGUISE

If we have found people who can push us in these areas, (since we oftentimes will not challenge ourselves to the extent that we need to be challenged), they are people to honor and treasure. *They are not being mean.* They are putting the pressure on us that will cause the diamond to emerge.

> Obey those who rule over you, and be submissive, for they watch out for your souls, as those who must give account. Let them do so with joy and not with grief, for that would be unprofitable for you (Hebrews 13:17).

Open rebuke is better than love carefully concealed. Faithful are the wounds of a friend, but the kisses of an enemy are deceitful (Proverbs 27:5-6).

Trainers are not often nice, but are some of the few who truly care (in word and deed) about whether we discover and experience our full potential. Providing an atmosphere of honor for them will make the process of our transformation much quicker and less painful for us (and them).

"DEALING WITH RESISTANCE" REVIEW

1. We have _____ _____limits which are barriers to our training in the spirit.

2. What is the number one barrier to effective training?

   _____

   What attitude (sin) does this show in the one being trained?

   _____

   _____

3. *Why should it be exciting and good when we sense these barriers and frustrations when we are being trained?*

   _____

   _____

4. We have to know the end goal and _____ through the resistance of the prison of the flesh and soul.

5. Only the Holy Spirit who made us really _____ who we are. When we feel_____in the process, it is just the fire of God bringing up the junk in our flesh and our souls. Keep _____!

6. _____ forces us to push to the point of breakthrough, releasing the strength of our spirits.

7. The resistance of others caused Bartimaeus to _____ release a greater cry of faith.

8. Resistance can be a _____-_____ to build and release the strength necessary to breakthrough to our miracles.

9. At which points in the training thus far have you felt the greatest resistance?

_____

_____

_____

What does this feeling and intensity of resistance in these areas mean for you?

_____

Conversely, if you *haven't* felt any resistance in some certain areas of the training thus far, what could *this* imply concerning you and the quality of your efforts in training?

_____

10. Resistance means we are entering a place of _____. God has a reward for us because He rewards overcomers (see Rev. 21:7).

PRACTICAL TRAINING

Revisit some of the exercises that have seemed too easy for you. How can you increase the intensity and challenge of these exercises in order to get a greater breakthrough?

Get a trainer! Find someone who has greater strength in a certain area of this training, and get that person to push you a bit more and challenge you. And you must be accountable to your trainer. Watch your attitude and keep a healthy respect for how your trainer is trying to help you. Remind that person to keep pushing you when things are getting comfortable for you!

Take note of your new results!

CHAPTER 13

RELEASING OUR SPIRITS

"And Jesus cried out again with a loud voice, and yielded up His spirit" (Matthew 27:50).

This brings us to the final part of this section of spirit life training. When Jesus was on the cross, it was the apex of His obedience. He had followed His Father's Will up to this final moment when all the forces of evil were pressing against Him. He felt alone, rejected, and abandoned. His flesh was totally broken and tormented. It was Jesus' darkest hour. But even in the darkest hour of His life, He still had a secret weapon. It was something no one could take away from Him. They took His friends, His justice, His dignity, His clothes, His health, His peace; but there was something He had molded and trained from day one that no one could take (see Luke 2:40). *It was His spirit.* He had kept it pure and strong for this hour of the greatest darkness.

STARTING A CHAIN REACTION OF THE MIRACULOUS

The devil didn't even realize that this was coming. The devil gleefully saw that Jesus' flesh was crushed and His soul was tortured. But suddenly, from beneath His flesh and soul exploded a spirit so mighty that shockwaves were sent throughout space and time.

> *Then, behold, the veil of the temple was torn in two from top to bottom; and the earth quaked, and the rocks were split, and the graves were opened; and many bodies of the saints who had fallen asleep were raised; and coming out of the graves after His resurrection, they went into the holy city and appeared to many. So when the centurion and those with him, who were guarding Jesus, saw the earthquake and the things that had happened, they feared greatly, saying, "Truly this was the Son of God!"* (Matthew 27:51-54)

At this moment, when Jesus released His spirit, a chain reaction of the miraculous took place. This is the final part of this training—this apex point at which we develop the ability to freely release our spirits when we need to. This is the place where we want to live. Let's slow this chain reaction down and let the Word of God show how this happens.

CHOOSING TO YIELD OUR SPIRITS TO GOD

"Jesus cried out again with a loud voice, and yielded up His spirit" (Matt. 27:50). This is when we fully live with our flesh reckoned dead to self (and sin) and a slave to God's Will (see Rom. 6:5-14). Our souls are fully submitted to God's Will as well (see Eph. 4:23). With these fully aligned, our spirits are poised to be released the moment we open our mouths. When we speak, it is with a voice of authority that splits the heavens. It is a voice that blasts away all obstacles that stand in the path of the Will of God being done. It is a voice and cry of freedom that declares with finality, *"It is finished!"* even before the physical events have outworked themselves to completion.

RELEASING OUR SPIRITS IN OUR VOICES

In John 11, it tells of Lazarus dying. Lazarus was Jesus' friend, and in the midst of that foul atmosphere of soulish sorrow and unbelief, Jesus made the decision to tap into the strength of His spirit (see John 11:33,38). After this intense groaning and locking fully into the strength of His spirit, He then rose up and said *"Take away the stone"* (John 11:39a). He spoke with such finality that they couldn't comprehend it. They couldn't see or understand that He had already released His spirit to the Father and that this miracle was as good as done. So then He revealed to them, through an open prayer, the fact that God had already heard Him—through the disciplined ability to release His spirit in the midst of unbelief and resistance.

> *Now when He had said these things, He cried out with a loud voice, "Lazarus, come forth!" And he who had died came out bound hand and foot with graveclothes, and his face was wrapped with a cloth. Jesus said to them, "Loose him and let him go"* (John 11:43-44).

This is the power available when we fully yield our flesh and souls over to God. We don't care what others think; we are totally focused on making the quality decision to release our spirits in word and deed. In everything we do, it is done with the focus and faith that our spirits are breaking out upon all of it. Sometimes it takes that loud cry to shatter all resistance in prayer. Or it takes that groaning within ourselves as we tap into the wisdom and will of God to know precisely what to do. These actions lock down and quarantine any fears and limitations of the flesh and soul so they don't taint the purity of our spirits' determination to make our bodies walk on the waters of the impossible. When our spirits are fully released, fear is a thousand miles away. There is a spiritual fire released upon us that saturates us with love, focus, purity, and energy to rise up and obey. There is a "knowing" of what to do (and what *not* to do), how to do it, and when to do it. That "knowing" also understands what will happen *after* we obey. This fills us with joy and excitement as we ride the wave of our spirits' release further along this chain reaction of events.

LET THE PRESENCE OF GOD RUSH IN

"Then, behold, the veil of the temple was torn in two from top to bottom..." (Matt. 27:51). After we release our spirits, God releases His presence. The Bible refers to a veil as a fleshly barrier, or limitation, blocking people from seeing or entering the Will and presence of God. In the temple, this veil prevented God's presence from breaking out on the people. But when Jesus released His spirit, God Himself took the initiative to tear down this barrier between people and Himself. When we release our spirits, God tears the fleshly veils from people's eyes and minds and His presence begins to break out upon them. Before, their flesh could try to stop what was happening or deny that He is real, but after we release our spirits, God reveals Himself to the people who surround us in unmistakable ways, showing that He is *real* and He is *here*.

IMPOSSIBILITIES SHIFT, SHAKE, AND SHATTER

"...And the earth quaked, and the rocks were split..." (Matt. 27:51). After the revealing of God's presence, the impossible, immovable situations will shift and shatter. The earth represents conditions that we have learned to live with. Rocks represent hard, impossible situations. No one can hide from an earthquake. It comes suddenly, and there is nowhere to run from it. Everything that seemed to be solid and unchangeable shifts and shatters. Obstacles that stood in the way

are no longer there. Everything is changed. The true secret to moving mountains is learning to release our spirits.

NEW LIFE IS BIRTHED

and the graves were opened; and many bodies of the saints who had fallen asleep were raised; and coming out of the graves after His resurrection, they went into the holy city and appeared to many (Matthew 27:52-53).

When we learn to release our spirits, we release *life.* "*It is the Spirit who gives life; the flesh profits nothing. The words that I speak to you are spirit, and they are life*" (John 6:63). There are people all around us every day who are asleep to hope, asleep to destiny, asleep to God. Maybe they were alive to these things at one time, but now they are dead and buried.

Death seems so unchangeable and irreversible. Once death has been accepted and the dead buried, the story seems over. But there is such a power inherent within the spirit that has been trained, strengthened, charged, and released by God that even dead things are restored to life and vibrancy. People's spirits are jumpstarted and come out of the graves of their flesh and souls to truly start to live. A new hope and brightness comes to their eyes. They come alive to worship and alive to a living relationship with God. They are disgusted with dead tradition and want nothing to do with it anymore. This thing is not done secretly, either; other people see and *know* these have come to life! We can't hide life.

THE REVELATION OF THE SONS OF GOD

...Now when the centurion and those with him, were guarding Jesus, saw the earthquake and the things that had happened,

they feared greatly saying, "Truly this was the Son of God" (Matthew 27:54).

When the chain reaction caused by the releasing of our spirits fully takes its course, the people who doubted us will finally stand back and admit that we are born of God. When we can govern our spirits to release them, the atmosphere around our lives will be saturated with the glory of God. We have a treasure in our earthen vessel. To be able to release it to a world that needs it will show them that God does truly dwell with us. He will be a Father, and we are revealed as His sons and daughters.

The world puts pressure on us because it demands that we must not keep that life for ourselves; we must release it (see Rom. 8:18-19). Paul made sure that he did not come to show his excellence of singing, suits, speech, knowledge, or looks. He came to serve the purposes of God for his generation by releasing his spirit—no matter if he was in the pulpit or the prison. *"For God is my witness, **whom I serve with my spirit** in the gospel of His Son..."* (Rom. 1:9).

NO BOUNDARIES IN THE SPIRIT

We have already seen that our spirits are much bigger than our natural bodies. *"You are of God little children, and have overcome them, because He who is in you is greater than he who is in the world"* (1 John 4:4). We think that since our spirits live in our natural bodies, they must be contained within our natural bodies. This is not true. This Scripture shows us that our capacity is much greater than what our physical bodies appear to possess. It is possible, through the conscious choice to release our spirits, for the nature of our spirits to fill a room and beyond.

We have all seen how one person's attitude can affect a room positively or negatively. This is the effect of the soul on other souls. But there is something deeper and stronger in the release of the human spirit. Through lining up our minds, Wills, and emotions with the Word of God and choosing to believe that what is in us is greater than anything contrary that is around us, we begin to affect the people and other spirits (demonic or angelic) in the room. Sometimes without even saying a word, our very presence exudes faith and confidence in the goodness of God. Our greeting causes evil forces to react, hide, or leave, and people's conversations turn toward the things of God. This happens because our spirits are greater than our physical bodies. We can (in a sense) "send them ahead of us" into the room or the house we are about to enter. Where we are focusing our souls (based on the Word and sensitivity to the Spirit of God), our spirits can move into that situation and begin to do a supernatural work.

This fact is real, but it must not be taken out of context with the rest of this book. Those who have been involved in witchcraft and other dark arts have seen the counterfeits of this through demonic power, but the Spirit of God in a person demonstrates the genuine reality of this purpose we were created for. When we start truly believing First John 4:4, we can truly start changing the world. It is sad that Christianity has been relegated to simply trying to change ourselves when the Word of God puts this life in the spirit at the level of *influencing the entire world*. Our spirits can rise, expand, and be released to go ahead of us into that hospital room and begin to bring an atmosphere for healing. Our spirits can be stirred up to saturate a household of strife and cause the peace of God to take dominion and reign in that place. Our spirits can look through our eyes into the tortured souls of hate across the room and cause them to weaken and melt by the force of the love of God flowing straight from us into them. The Spirit of truth can produce such an influence through our presence that the lying tongue will be silenced in our children or even our business partners.

Where we focus to release our spirits, we release the supernatural ability of God to do what our flesh and souls are powerless to do. *There are things that our flesh is designed to do and that our souls are designed to do and that our spirits are designed to do.* We cannot substitute the flesh and soul to try to do what only the spirit was designed to do. Only our spirits have the power to address the primary needs of humankind. The spirit must go first. Oh the hours and years we have wasted in our lives, trying to force the tools of flesh and soul to do the work that the spirit could prepare and do effectively in a few moments! God gave you a spirit for a reason.

Release it.

Let it go before you.

Let it take dominion.

Use its strength and ability to do the will of God in the earth.

It all begins with your choice.

In all of our spirit life training, let our goal be to do whatever is necessary to release our spirits into a world that needs to see the living God.

"RELEASING OUR SPIRITS" REVIEW

1. No one could take away Jesus' _____ because He had kept it pure and strong for this hour of greatest darkness. We need to know we have the ability to release our spirits when we need to—no matter what we are facing.

2. When we release our spirits, we start a _____-_____ of the miraculous.

3. Jesus releasing His spirit on the cross is an example to us of our flesh _____ _____ ___ ____, and our souls are _____ _____ to _____ _____. With these fully aligned, our spirits are poised to be released the moment we _____ _____ _____.

4. The _____ of our spirits speaks with a cry of _____ and finality that "____ ____ _____," even before the physical events have _____ _____ ___ _____.

5. We have the privilege of making a quality _____ to release our spirits with our _____ and_____.

6. In everything we do, it is done with a _____ and _____ that our spirits are _____ _____ upon all of it!

7. When our spirits are fully released, _____ is a thousand miles away. A spiritual fire is released that saturates us with love, focus, purity, and energy to rise up and obey. There is a "_____" of what to do and how and when to do it. We know what will happen after we obey.

8. The first thing that happens when we release our spirits is that God releases His tangible _____ into that place. People will know that God is _____ and He is _____!

9. The second thing we can expect when we release our spirits is that the impossible, immovable situations begin to _____ and _____.

10. The true secret to moving mountains is to learn to _____ _____ _____!

11. The third thing that occurs when we release our spirits is that we release _____ (see John 6:63).

    What kind of effects will this have on people and situations around us?

    _____

    _____

12. When we can _____ and release our spirits, the fourth effect will be that the atmosphere around our lives will be _____ with the glory of God.

13. God will be revealed as a _____, and we will be revealed as true _____ and _____ of Him.

14. Our _____ have a much greater capacity than what our physical bodies appear to possess (see 1 John 4:4).

15. A person's _____ can affect a room positively or negatively. But there is something _____ and _____ in the release of the human spirit.

16. When we _____ ____ our minds, emotions, and Wills with the _____ ___ _____ and choosing to _____ that what is in us is greater than _____ _____ ____ ____ that is around us, *what effects will this have?*

17. Based on First John 4:4, what are we able to do, even when we are not in a certain location yet?

18. There are things that our _____ is designed to do, things that our _____ are designed to do, and things that our _____ are designed to do. We cannot substitute the _____ and _____ to try to do what only the _____ was meant to do.

19. Only our spirits have the power to address the _____ _____ of humankind. The spirit must go first. God gave each of us a spirit for a reason! It all begins with our *choice!*

PRACTICAL TRAINING

This is the most important point of this section of the training. *Everything thus far leads up to this.*

Make sure to use what you learned and experienced in the previous exercises as it will become important for this next practical training step. Otherwise, this will seem like acting rather than a real spiritual exercise.

Plan to find five experiences in the next few days in which you make the conscious choice to release your spirit in those situations.

Make note of the preparation, poise, and release process of your spirit in these situations. (Make sure you are experiencing something similar to question 7 above!) *Expect the four results of the release of the spirit into that situation.* Write notes on the lead-up to the situation and how this process happened and any results you noticed right away. (For abbreviated examples, see page 220.)

Example:

1)

   a. *Situation:*

_____

_____

b. *How you know you released your spirit:*

_____

_____

c. *Noticeable results:*

_____

_____

1)

a.

_____

_____

b.

_____

_____

c.

_____

_____

2)

a.

_____

_____

b.

_____

_____

c.

_____

_____

3)

   a.

_____

_____

   b.

_____

_____

   c.

_____

_____

4)

   a.

_____

_____

   b.

_____

_____

   c.

_____

_____

5)

   a.

_____

_____

   b.

_____

_____

C.

_____

_____

PART II

RELATIONSHIP WITH THE HOLY SPIRIT

CHAPTER 14

ACTION STEPS FOR RELATIONSHIP

I want to start off with a powerful statement worthy of continual memorization and meditation: *"The Holy Spirit has nothing better to do than to have a relationship with you."*

During this training thus far, I have mostly dealt with spirit, soul, and body issues. This is foundational, but it leads into something more personal—knowing the Holy Spirit as a separate entity from our spirits. He is not just a force of God or a mechanism that makes God do things in our lives. The Holy Spirit is our Teacher, Helper, Friend, Leader, and more. Once these spirit, soul, and body issues are addressed and exercised, it is easier to develop this important relationship aspect of our spirit life.

What brings Christianity out of the realm of religion is the relationship we can have with God. He really talks with us. He really teaches us. He really, intimately *knows* us! We don't have to wait until we've perfectly trained our spirits, souls, and bodies to start developing this relationship; everything is an ongoing process. But it is important to understand that Jesus called *disciples* to follow Him first! Before He introduced them to the Holy Spirit, He had to work with people who understood the importance of disciplining their souls and bodies. *Anyone with experience in relationships knows that it is difficult (or even impossible) to develop quality relationships with people who have no discipline in their lives.*

The Holy Spirit will *not* force us to do anything. He will not force us to hear His voice; He will not force us to obey Him; He will not force us to be good students. He *could,* but that would violate His desire to have a quality relationship. Believe it or not, there are principles to having quality relationships! This quality relationship must be based on love from both sides. This means that each side of the relationship truly wants the other side to be blessed and have the best. They will sacrifice whatever is necessary for the other's betterment.

This relationship must be offered and desired from both sides of the relationship. There must be openness in communication. Both sides must be able to express themselves freely on the basis of truth, neither trying to deceive the other. There must also be integrity in communication. In order to strengthen a sense of unity, they have to experience that what others say they will do, they will do. That way both sides will be able to discover and trust how the other thinks consistently.

There must also be regularity in communication. The more frequently communication occurs, the more the two sides share their lives. This results in a further blending of the two lives. There must also be a sense of delight, honor, and respect for each other. Even though they are starting to discover each other more and more, they still understand that the other party is separate, special, and a treasure that must be valued. Once the sense of value is lost, the gifts that they possess can no longer be transferred into each other's lives.

These are some basic principles, and we could study them more in depth, but I want to make this training more practical. So I will *give some action steps that incorporate these principles* so we can get started in this wonderful relationship with the Holy Spirit.

1. BELIEVE HE IS NEAR US

He may be invisible, but the danger is to ignore Him! This was the foolishness of Jacob. *"Then Jacob awoke from his sleep and said, 'Surely the Lord is in this place and I did not know it'"* (Gen. 28:16).

The key is to *believe.* When we say continually, "I *know* You are near me, Holy Spirit," and we believe it when we say it, something happens in the atmosphere of our hearts. Our spirits awaken and our beings are poised and positioned for Him to do or say something. This is so important to get into the *habit* of doing this *wherever we are.* This habit is called developing a "God-consciousness." It doesn't change the Holy Spirit at all, but it does change our mental focus, which keeps the channel open for the Holy Spirit to speak to our spirits and our spirits to immediately connect those thoughts and experiences to our minds.

Practice His Presence

Brother Lawrence wrote a classic called, *The Practice of the Presence of God.* This 17th century monk decided to believe that God was with him everywhere and participating with him in everything he did, from washing the dishes and working in the garden to praying and praising God. He would commune with God *everywhere.* He would ask Him questions and turn his mind to God and His love continually. What was he doing? He was *training* himself to be God-conscious. This God consciousness will help us develop a relationship with the Holy Spirit *everywhere,* not just in church or the prayer room.

The training goes like this:

- When we are at work, we break our old habits and start thanking Him that He is with us in our cubicle *right now.*

- Thank Him that He is walking into that business meeting *right now.*

- Thank Him that He is pumping gas with us at the gas station *right now.*

- Thank Him that He is eating fast food with us *right now.*

- Thank Him that He is encountering that friend with us at the mall *right now.*

- Thank Him that He is standing and waiting at our bedsides when we wake up *right now.*

We need to expand our minds to think of the strangest or most ordinary situations we find ourselves in from day to day and recognize the reality is that He is *right there*—and He is waiting to be acknowledged. *He is activated when He is acknowledged.* Let's read that over and over again until it is burned into our memories. It can't be said often enough.

He Always Has Time for Us

Remember this profound truth: The Holy Spirit *has nothing better to do* than to have relationship with us. When we open our hearts to acknowledge His presence, we are participating with His top priority of His day. He is not human; He is not limited by time and space. He does not value His relationship with one person over another. He *always* has time for all of us! People may not, but He has all the time in the world for us. In fact, He is the one who gives us our time. Do we have time *for Him*? We must share every part of our days with Him.

2. DON'T BE AFRAID OF WHAT HE SAYS

The first action step is so simple; it seems that everyone should know and do it. In theory everyone will say that it's true. But most don't practice His presence at all. Why is that? Let's look at Psalm 27:4:

One thing I have desired of the Lord, that I will seek: that I may dwell in the house of the Lord all the days of my life, to behold the beauty of the Lord, and to inquire in His temple.

This is talking about experiencing God's presence every day of our lives. David says that he does this for two reasons. First, he wanted to see God's beauty. Second, he wanted to ask Him questions! I wanted to make "asking Him questions" action step 2. However, there is a reason people don't ask Him questions; it is the same reason they don't want to acknowledge His presence. *They are afraid of what He will say.*

Never Doubt; He Is a Good God

This goes way back to the sin-consciousness that Adam and Eve had when they tried to hide from God (see Gen. 3:8). The moment they heard Him or thought about Him being near, it awakened a fear that they had to hide from Him (of course we can't really hide from Him). Oftentimes people think God will always disapprove of their actions, lives, or thoughts. They think God will ruin their whole lives by what He says. There is a very real fear that they have wasted their entire lives, while thinking that they were doing the right thing. They think God will start opening up the list of all their shortcomings and then criticize them for waiting so long to come to Him. They would rather be blissfully ignorant than risk the chance that God might hurt their feelings by what He says.

This kind of thinking is wrong. It is true that God knows every mistake we have made. But He is not going to crush us with that information! *God is good.* Even in the Garden of Eden, after Adam and Eve sinned, God was good to them. He *knew they had sinned,* but He *still* came to have fellowship with them! Adam knew he was naked and that he had sinned, but God asked him a curious question. *"Who told you that you were naked?"* God should have been the one to condemn, but it was Adam who condemned himself. So what did God do about it? He implemented a plan to deliver people from their sins. Everything God says is to lift us up and give us a way out.

> No temptation has overtaken you except such as is common to man; but God is faithful, who will not allow you to be tempted beyond what you are able, but with the temptation will also make the way of escape, that you may be able to bear it (1 Corinthians 10:13).

What is the way of escape? *He* is the way of escape. His first mission is to *save* us!

Recognize and Resist the Voice of Fear

When we get into the habit of pausing and simply acknowledging, "Holy Spirit, thank You for being here *right now*," the sense of His presence will be refreshed to us immediately. Then we can start asking Him questions. Ask Him *anything*. He will tell us what we need to know. *But at the same time, we must not be afraid* of what He will say to us! Fear cuts off our ability to hear God's voice. The voice of fear is the devil's voice. Know that.

As we read through the Bible, something very interesting happens whenever God shows up to talk to someone. He will start off by saying, "Don't be afraid." He starts off that way because *unless fear is dealt with first, we won't be able to hear anything else He has to say!* When He comes to talk, He comes to help. When we open our hearts to talk to Him, He will not discourage us for that. *If we knew how many times His voice could have saved us in the past, we would cry.* He wants us to forget the past mistakes and to work with Him *starting now*.

The wise *love* correction; fools despise it. So what *if* He says something that corrects us? Is that for our hurt or our help? Obviously it is for our help. So we must embrace *whatever* He says. When we open up,

His voice will bring us true freedom. The word He speaks to us is going to be the exact word we need. *Expect it.*

Expect Him to Say Something

Some may say, "What if I'm afraid that He *won't* speak to me?" This is another very real issue. This is a fear we have to crush. Jesus clearly says in John 10 three different times that His sheep will know His voice. When we choose to give our lives to Him, He puts inside us all of the technology we need to hear Him. We have to believe that. The key is this: After we acknowledge Him and ask Him something, we must *expect* Him to say something! A clear thought will pop into our minds that has a unique authority. It will be in line with Scripture, and it will have the heart of a father in it. Once this thought comes, we accept it and pray about how to apply it accurately.

We must not be careless with what we hear. Once we lose that sense of honor for His voice, our ability to hear becomes less clear. When He speaks, we should write it down and *remember* it. Sometimes it won't make sense right away. But later on, it will. We just need to know that He speaks what He speaks for a good reason. We have to expect it!

Supernatural, but Ordinary—and Needed

We must understand that He will sometimes speak something very ordinary, something not very "spiritual" at all, something like "tie your shoes" or "compliment this person," and so forth. What we don't understand—that the Holy Spirit does—is that small triggers fire big guns. It could be that small step of obedience in listening that makes a huge difference in our lives and someone else's. It could start a chain reaction that leads to great opportunities; we just need to trust Him!

Make His Voice a Habitual Dependency

We must learn to embrace His voice as a habit. There will be times when the pressure is great, and if we haven't mastered overcoming the fear of His voice (or fear of lacking it) during those times, it will be next to impossible to hear Him when fear caused by a situation is screaming the loudest. Instead, we must train ourselves daily to shut that fear down and determine according to His Word, *"I will stand my watch and set myself on the rampart, and watch to see what He will say to me..."* (Hab. 2:1).

Determine to hear. God spoke to me before, *"What the world is waiting for is for someone who can simply hear My voice."* Isn't that the truth? Of all the skills we may have, won't this be the most valuable for life?

3. PERFECT OUR SKILLS TO INTENSIFY HIS PRESENCE

We are all unique. The Bible says that we were created for His good pleasure (see Rev. 4:11; Eph. 1:3-9). *We can each touch His heart in a way that no one else can.* This action step is a bit trickier than others because it requires a lover's skill.

The Art of Romance

Believe it or not, inside all of us is some kind of romantic ability. It's not the physical lust of some soap opera or romance film. It's simply an ability to recognize and respond to what another person likes. We see people we want to get to know better. We try to put away all our flaws and "put our best foot forward." We find out what they like and make an effort to give them that or talk about that. We make ourselves vulnerable and open. We choose our words wisely, wanting to use the words that draw them out. We enjoy and value what they say and laugh at their jokes. We bring them to places and situations that they would enjoy and where they can be free to express themselves. We are happy when they are happy. We plan and give surprises to them that they would enjoy. We go out of our way to protect and provide for them. We want everything we do to inspire their trust in our sincere love for them. We sacrifice for them because their love for us is more valuable than what we have to sacrifice.

These are all skills that we discover in ourselves when we want to pursue a relationship. They may not be perfected right away, but the desire for intimacy provides the drive to keep trying.

We Love to See Him Happy

The Holy Spirit is a lover. He can be "turned on" in a sense. The reason I say that is because the Bible says that His presence can be quenched (see 1 Thess. 5:19) or grieved (see Eph. 4:30). This implies the emotional attachment He has to us. The Bible also talks about being *full* of the Holy Spirit, literally intoxicated with Him (see Eph. 5:18). This means that we are so consumed and intimate with Him that He fills our beings at all times.

The Holy Spirit loves people. But not all people love the Holy Spirit. What can He do about that? He knows that any relationship that is going to be valued must be pursued, so He will draw people to know Him. But we must also make the effort to perfect our skills and principles of romance on Him to experience Him more fully. The Bible does give some guidance for how this can be accomplished.

First, the Holy Spirit loves *response*. When we perfect the first two action steps (believing He is near and choosing to not be afraid of what He says), we come to a place where we start to sense what He is doing or going to do. We then respond to what He says or shows right away, not as a slave or a robot, but as someone in love. We love to make Him happy. He knows when we do it for that reason. This intensifies His presence.

> *Therefore, as the Holy Spirit says: "Today, if you will hear His voice, do not harden your hearts as in the rebellion, in the day of trial in the wilderness..." (Hebrews 3:7-8).*

We give when He tells us to give; we go where He tells us to go; we speak what He tells us to speak; we are moved with the same emotions that move Him. The closer our actions, attitudes, and emotions mirror His, the more strongly we experience His presence.

Responding to the "Inward Witness"

How do we know whether or not we are responding properly to Him? We get this small sensation on the inside. It could be called an "inward witness." This sensation is best described as a "yes, go ahead" feeling, or a "no, don't do it" feeling or a "be very alert, proceed carefully" feeling deep on the inside. Sometimes this is termed the "green, red, and yellow lights" of the Spirit's guidance, relating to our understanding of traffic lights. After we experience this sensation in the midst of a situation, then a choice must be made: do we respond with it or ignore it? If we respond, it gets stronger, clearer, and more intense. If we ignore it, it will twist up our insides for a moment, but soon it will go away. But we are left feeling empty. That's called "hardening our hearts."

The best choice is to respond to His leading. Again, it will be in line with the Scriptures, and the action will be motivated by the love of God. Also, the action doesn't have to be weird or complex. It can be very simple. I believe most times it is simple. Everything He wants us to do, He knows we will be good at.

Simple Songs of Love

Another thing that the Holy Spirit likes is when we *sing* to Him. He is a true romantic!

> ...*be filled with the Spirit, speaking to one another in psalms and hymns and spiritual songs, singing and making melody in your heart to the Lord, giving thanks always for all things to God the Father in the name of our Lord Jesus Christ* (Ephesians 5:18-20).

It doesn't matter if our voices win any prizes or not; there is something about expressing our love to Him in a song or a melody. He knows what we are trying to do. He will sometimes give us the words to draw Him near. True, it's not a surprise to Him then, but then again, what is? As we sing the words He gives us, He loves the fact that we are listening and responding to Him, letting our beings resonate with His voice. It causes Him to intensify His presence.

Lifting Voices With Strength and Revelation

The key is this: We must mean what we are singing! The Bible says to *"sing to the Lord a new song!"* (Ps. 98:1), because the trap is, if we know a song really well, we start to be able to sing it out of habit instead of truly meaning it afresh to Him. He knows when we are sincere or not. The angels of God can sing the same song over and over to Him because they mean it more and more every single time they sing it!

Moving With the Holy Spirit

One level beyond singing is dancing for Him. I know that this may be even more difficult to understand, but the Holy Spirit likes dancing, especially when it is for Him. When King David was bringing the ark to Jerusalem, he went before it and was dancing with all his might before the Lord. David's wife was watching him and was ashamed at this display. When he got home, happy and tired, she then began to scold him for his behavior. But David simply explained,

> It was before the Lord, who chose me instead of your father and all his house, to appoint me ruler over the people of the Lord, over Israel. Therefore I will play music before the Lord. And I will be even more undignified than this, and will be humble in my own sight... (2 Samuel 6:21-22).

David was so thankful for what God had done for him that he had to dance and play music to express his gratitude and praise. The Holy

Spirit loved that expressive fruit of intimacy toward Him. When Michal (David's wife) lashed out at it, the Holy Spirit reacted jealously by not giving her any children (the fruit of intimacy) of her own. See, it was not just a simple dance; it was David skillfully intensifying the Spirit's presence through his romancing of Him. Some may think it is silly, but when our motive is to draw Him near by our dance, He is going to run to us! I'm not suggesting we do some seductive, fleshly dance moves; rather, let it be a dance of joy, of praise, of excitement! Let's let Him energize us and dance with us!

When We Are All Alone

These all can be very expressive and exuberant displays of affection. But there is another way to draw Him near. This is through secret displays of affection. There are things people do to show others that they love God. That's fine and good, but the Holy Spirit is with us when no one else sees. When we get alone with Him and whisper to Him or do some kind of secret sacrifice to bless Him, He responds to that. Jesus constantly talked about *"...your Father who sees in secret, will reward you openly..."* (Matt. 6:4,6; see also Matt. 6:18). He spoke this regarding fasting, prayer, and giving. These are secret sacrifices of love that the Holy Spirit responds to. All sense of loneliness leaves us forever when we perfect this skill.

Whenever we get alone with Him, our minds automatically go to, *Hmmm...What can I do for Him right now? I want to let Him know I appreciate His presence so much!* We can do that with a whisper or a quiet song or by reaching up our hands to Him and pretending to hug Him. It may seem silly to us, but He knows what we mean and what we want. He will hug us right back! Our alone times thus become so saturated with His presence; *He is so real to us.* That is a reward in itself. *But out of that place, He will also magnify that reward so that everyone will know He thinks we're special.* He loves to be acknowledged and focused on. He wants to be our true love. We can't just tell Him, "Draw me close to You." *We must draw **Him** close to us!* Instead of being apathetic lovers, we must be romancers. Our voices should be so drawing that the moment He hears us, it seems He would run from the other side of the world to get to us! If we can perfect our romance skills toward Him, His presence will intensify around our lives and He will do anything to defend our honor.

4. FIND A PLACE TO BE WITH HIM

This may seem contradictory from the first action step. We must know and acknowledge that He is everywhere. But to be able to build intimacy, we also need a place where there are no distractions, where we can just be with Him alone. This action step leads directly from the last one because we also need a private place where we can practice and perfect these romance skills.

Birthplace of Relationship

Jesus had places He would go to be alone with His Father—the wilderness, the mountaintop, a garden, and so forth (see Luke 5:16; Matt. 14:23; Luke 22:39). Moses built a tabernacle of meeting just to be alone with God (see Exod. 33:7). Elijah would go to Mount Horeb to hear His still small voice (see 1 Kings 19:8). Daniel had a regular place where he would get down on his knees and pray toward Jerusalem (see Dan. 6:10).

I have spent time in Muslim countries and have been very impressed at their respect for prayer. In almost every building—it doesn't matter if it is a mall, airport, shop, supermarket, restaurant, sports arena, or office building—they have simple rooms set aside solely for prayer. Quite frankly, I am a bit jealous. Sometimes I want to go somewhere where I can pray without distraction when I am out and about during my day. But can I do that in a mall in America? No! Can I do that in a restaurant in America? No! Perhaps in sports arenas (filled with those who had bet on the game maybe)? But not even there can I find a prayer room. Why do I bring this up? It's because of the casualness with which we treat the Holy Spirit.

True, He is everywhere. He does not live in buildings made by people's hands. *We* are His temple. I have already talked about that in the beginning of this training. *But* look at what we do and the attitude we have. We build rooms for guests. We build rooms for cars. We build rooms for entertainment. We build rooms for cooking food. We build rooms for eating. We build rooms for work. We build rooms for books. We even build rooms for hot tubs and pools. *But how many people designate* **one** *room to build a relationship with the most valuable person in our lives?* This must become a conviction that is so important to us that we can have a place where we walk in the door and *know*—He is there and that is all that matters. It is not shared by any other activity. It is simply a Holy Spirit saturation room. It is a place where we can pour out our hearts to Him and He can download into us without interruption. We can intercede, sing, declare, listen, and write. There is no bed, no television, no mirror, no phone, no refrigerator, no computer; He is the most important thing there. All of our senses must be focused solely on Him.

What Are We Missing?

We are one of the most advanced generations in many ways. We have so many things technologically working for our advantage. Those in the Book of Acts didn't have a fraction of what we do in these areas, *but* they had the Holy Spirit. They knew what it took to summon Him to come and shake the place. When we set aside a room without any of the gadgets that make our lives easier, we get back to what really is necessary to summon the presence of the Holy Spirit. We do all those things they didn't do (that we think will be a better way), but we don't do those things they did that really pleased the Holy Spirit!

When we set aside a room, we can concentrate with the same raw ingredients that they used—the Holy Spirit, us, our voices in prayer and praise, our love and desire for Him, our memories of what He has done, and our imagination of what He has promised. It is raw, but it is the place where miracles are birthed. In my travels, this was not always easy to have. But I knew that I needed a *place* where it was just me and Him. Sometimes I could find a room I could use; sometimes I had to walk out into a field or next to the ocean or even through a forest! The kind of places I found could be beautiful, strange, or sometimes uncomfortable.

Obsessed to Meet With Him

The key was that as soon as I started walking out to get alone with Him, He would meet me while I was walking. He would help me find a place and would bless me for taking the effort to do so. When I am traveling, I have to make time for this. My schedule would get changed around so much at times. *But my mind is bent on finding a place and a time that I can be alone with Him.* That's what I want. And I know that will not be taken away from me. I can choose to give it up, but I know *no one* but me can take it away (see Luke 10:42). God will make sure of that. So it is also important to schedule a time when we will meet with Him in that place. If we are regular in our appointments with Him, our anticipation builds to the point that once we step into the room, we will know He is waiting for us. Why not start now? Our true Trainer is ready to take us to the next level.

"ACTION STEPS FOR RELATIONSHIP" REVIEW

1. The Holy Spirit has _____ _____ to do than have a relationship with us!

2. The Holy Spirit is a _____ _____ from our spirits. He is our _____, _____, _____, _____, and more.

3. Jesus called _____ to follow Him first before He introduced them to the Holy Spirit.

   Why is it important to have discipline in our lives in order to maintain strong relationships?

   _____

   _____

4. A quality relationship must:

   1) Be based on _____ from both sides.

   2) Be _____ and _____ from both sides.

   3) Be _____ in communication.

   4) Have _____ in communication.

   5) Have _____ in communication.

   6) Reveal a sense of _____, _____ and _____ for each other.

5. Discuss how each of the above six principles is relevant to our relationship with the Holy Spirit:

   1) _____

   2) _____

3) _____

4) _____

5) _____

6) _____

Believe He Is Near

6. The key is to _____ He is near and say, "____ _____ you are near me, Holy Spirit."

7. Make it a habit of _____ His presence; commune with Him in everything _____ _____!

8. He is _____ when He is _____.

PRACTICAL TRAINING STEP

Write down the full statement in question number one on a few note cards and put them in places you see regularly through-out your day (i.e., your desk, sink, counter, car, mirror). Let this remind you of this truth and spur you to do number 8. (Change the locations of the notes after a couple weeks.) Thank Him for this, then open up and invite the Holy Spirit to get involved with what you are doing!

Note at least three situations in which you noticed the difference this makes:

1) _____

2) _____

3) _____

Don't Be *Afraid* of What He Says

9. _____ His presence and _____ _____ _____.

   People who don't ask are _____ of what He will say.

10. Recognize the voice of fear and _____ it! Fear cuts off our
    ability to hear God's voice.

11. Embrace _____ He says. Expect His Word to be what
    you need. After you acknowledge Him and ask Him something,
    _____ Him to say something in response!

12. Listen and _____ what He says, even though it may seem
    ordinary; _____ to hear Him.

PRACTICAL TRAINING STEP

Note four ordinary questions that you asked the Holy Spirit throughout your day. After listening, note the response that you sensed. (Some responses don't come immediately; remember the questions you asked and be alert for the exact moment when the response comes!)

QUESTIONS	RESPONSES
1) _____	_____
2) _____	_____
3) _____	_____
4) _____	_____

Perfect Our Skills to Intensify His Presence

13. _____ starts with the ability to recognize and respond to what another person likes.

14. The Holy Spirit is a _____! He loves people and will draw them to Himself, but we must make the effort to _____ ____ _____ and principles of _____ on Him to experience Him more fully.

15. First, the Holy Spirit loves _____. The _____ our actions, attitudes, and emotions mirror His, the _____ His presence becomes.

16. When we get an "inward witness," we must choose to _____. If we _____it, we will start hardening our hearts. Don't be afraid! What He wants us to do, He knows we'll be _____ at.

17. The Holy Spirit likes us to _____ to Him (see Eph. 5:18b-20). Sing the words _____ _____ ____ _____. He loves the fact that we are listening and responding to Him; let's let our beings resonate with His voice. It causes Him to intensify His presence.

18. The key is to _____ what we are singing! He knows whether we are sincere or not.

19. A level beyond singing is _____. In Second Samuel 6:21-22, David was so thankful for what God had done for him that he had to dance and play music to express his gratitude and praise.

20. Dance is an expression of joy, praise, and excitement; we must let Him _____ us and dance with us!

21. The _____ _____ of love that the Holy Spirit responds to are fasting, prayer, and giving.

22. How and why does every sense of loneliness leave us forever?

23. Let's let our voices be so _____ that the moment He hears us, it's like He would run from the other side of the world to get to us!

PRACTICAL TRAINING STEP

This will flow in combination with the other two training steps. After you have done step one and two, *respond* in love to the Holy Spirit in some fashion. Be a little silly and vulnerable by doing each one of the examples in this step. Be appropriate to the situation, but sneak as many of these in as possible during the day. As a part of building a new habit, your commitment is to do at least ten separate instances per day. But you *must* do it to love *Him* or else it doesn't count. Keep record and put the amount under each day below. *You must try each one!*

Examples: Sensitivity, response, gifts, simple displays to please Him, singing, dancing, whispering, hugs, thanks, giving, fasting, thinking thoughts about Him, skillful use of words and voice, sneaking away for a moment to talk to Him, and so forth.

Monday: _____

Tuesday: _____

Wednesday: _____

Thursday: _____

Friday: _____

Saturday: _____

Sunday: _____

Find a Place to Be With Him

24. We need a place where there are no _____, where we can be with Him alone.

    Why is this important?

25. Such a place can be a Holy Spirit _____ room where all of our senses can be focused solely on Him.

26. We need the time to be with Him and use our _____ in prayer and praise, love, and imagination of what He has promised so that we can remember what He has done and will do.

    How can our imaginations both prepare us and help us the moment we step into this place?

27. It is important to _____ a time with the Holy Spirit so we can anticipate meeting Him there—and He will be there.

28. What is God's promise to us concerning this? (See Luke 10:41-42.)

PRACTICAL TRAINING STEP

Find a place! Use the tips and examples on pages 242-243 and start setting that place apart as sacred for this purpose of meeting with Him.

Meeting time! For the next week or two, build a regular pattern where you visit Him at that place at a specific time. Don't be late! If you are, apologize to Him. Build a pattern of faithfulness and honor for Him in your mind like you would for a scheduled meeting with a king or president.

Write the days and times below:

Monday: _____

Tuesday: _____

Wednesday: _____

Thursday: _____

Friday: _____

Saturday: _____

Sunday: _____

What to do? Use the tips in this step and practice the rest of the steps in this part of the book with more focus and fervency. Make sure you know what you are doing, that there is time when you know you are building your spirit and time when you are totally focused on the Holy Spirit with the strength you have built in your spirit through the alignment of your soul and body.

Take some specific dedicated time to do your part one exercises, but stay open to give the Holy Spirit complete permission to interrupt and direct you on how to train and emphasize each exercise more specifically for you for the glory of God. *As time progresses, the two parts will flow together seamlessly.*

Don't quit! Know that whatever you sow to the Spirit *will result* in life everlasting for you and others (see Gal. 6:8).

NOTES

ABOUT TIMOTHY JORGENSEN

For more information on *Spirit Life Training,* the ministry of Timothy Jorgensen, Spirit Life Training Seminars, and other helpful resources, please visit our Website at www.spiritlifetraining.com.

We look forward to hearing your testimonies!

Contact us at spiritlifetraining@gmail.com.

In the right hands, This Book will Change Lives!

Most of the people who need this message will not be looking for this book. To change their lives, you need to put a copy of this book in their hands.

> *But others (seeds) fell into good ground, and brought forth fruit, some a hundred-fold, some sixty-fold, some thirty-fold* (Matthew 13:8).

Our ministry is constantly seeking methods to find the good ground, the people who need this anointed message to change their lives. Will you help us reach these people?

> *Remember this—a farmer who plants only a few seeds will get a small crop. But the one who plants generously will get a generous crop* (2 Corinthians 9:6).

EXTEND THIS MINISTRY BY SOWING
3 BOOKS, 5 BOOKS, 10 BOOKS, OR MORE TODAY,
AND BECOME A LIFE CHANGER!

Thank you,

Don Nori Sr., Founder
Destiny Image
Since 1982